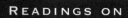

READINGS ON

BEOWULF

OTHER TITLES IN THE GREENHAVEN PRESS LITERARY COMPANION SERIES:

AMERICAN AUTHORS

Maya Angelou
Stephen Crane
Emily Dickinson
William Faulkner
F. Scott Fitzgerald
Nathaniel Hawthorne
Ernest Hemingway
Herman Melville
Arthur Miller
Eugene O'Neill
Edgar Allan Poe
John Steinbeck
Mark Twain
Thornton Wilder

BRITISH AUTHORS

Jane Austen
Joseph Conrad
Charles Dickens

WORLD AUTHORS

Fyodor Dostoyevsky
Homer
Sophocles

AMERICAN LITERATURE

The Adventures of
    Huckleberry Finn
The Catcher in the Rye
The Glass Menagerie
The Great Gatsby
Of Mice and Men
The Scarlet Letter

BRITISH LITERATURE

Animal Farm
The Canterbury Tales
Lord of the Flies
Romeo and Juliet
Shakespeare: The Comedies
Shakespeare: The Histories
Shakespeare: The Sonnets
Shakespeare: The Tragedies
A Tale of Two Cities

WORLD LITERATURE

The Diary of a Young Girl

THE GREENHAVEN PRESS
Literary Companion
TO BRITISH LITERATURE

READINGS ON

BEOWULF

David L. Bender, *Publisher*
Bruno Leone, *Executive Editor*
Brenda Stalcup, *Managing Editor*
Bonnie Szumski, *Series Editor*
Stephen P. Thompson, *Book Editor*

Greenhaven Press, San Diego, CA

Every effort has been made to trace the owners of copyrighted material. The articles in this volume may have been edited for content, length, and/or reading level. The titles have been changed to enhance the editorial purpose. Those interested in locating the original source will find the complete citation on the first page of each article.

Library of Congress Cataloging-in-Publication Data

Readings on Beowulf / Stephen P. Thompson, book editor.
        p.   cm. — (Greenhaven Press literary companion to British literature)
    Includes bibliographical references and index.
    ISBN 1-56510-813-2 (lib. : alk. paper). —
ISBN 1-56510-812-4 (pbk. : alk. paper)
    1. Beowulf. 2. Epic poetry, English (Old)—History and criticism. 3. Civilization, Anglo-Saxon, in literature.
4. Germanic peoples in literature. 5. Heroes in literature.
6. Rhetoric, Medieval. I. Thompson, Stephen P., 1953–   .
II. Series
PR1585.R43   1998
829'.3—dc21   97-43629
                                                                CIP

Copyright ©1998 by Greenhaven Press, Inc.
PO Box 289009
San Diego, CA 92198-9009
Printed in the U.S.A.

*66 Often many have to suffer
from the choice of one, as has
happened to us. We could not
give our king and protector
any good advice, or persuade
him not to approach the
guardian of the treasure-
hoard, but let the creature go
on living in its den till the
world's end. Beowulf held to
his destiny. . . . Harsh was the
doom that led our king here! 99*

Wiglaf in Beowulf
(Lines 3077–3086)

CONTENTS

Foreword 10

Introduction 12

The *Beowulf* Poet and His World 14

Chapter 1: Social and Cultural Context

1. *Beowulf* as a Heroic-Elegiac Poem *by J.R.R. Tolkien* 24
Beowulf is a unique epic poem; it is unfair to judge it by the standards of classical literary epic poems. *Beowulf* may be described best as both heroic, celebrating the amazing exploits of its hero, and elegiac, mourning the loss of such a hero and such a noble, exciting world.

2. Anglo-Saxon Language and Traditions in *Beowulf*
by Barry Tharaud 31
Beowulf was composed during an era of invasions and re-settlings of England. The Angles, Saxons, and Jutes who settled England brought with them not only their Germanic language but the central Germanic value perhaps best described as heroic excellence in battle, an excellence that involves strength, courage, and loyalty.

3. Heroic and Social Codes in *Beowulf*
by Howell D. Chickering Jr. 38
The most powerful motives for action in *Beowulf* are derived from the basic social unit of society, the king and his band of warriors. The loyalty between members of this group, involving their obligation to satisfy justice through a revenge code, is key to understanding the behavior of Beowulf and other main characters.

4. The Pessimism of Many Germanic Stories
by A. Kent Hieatt 45
The essence of loyalty in Germanic stories, including *Beowulf*, is the willingness to revenge wrongs done to any member of the group. Beowulf's own sense of loyalty conforms to this ethic, and there is no possibility of avoiding its hold. This principle of justice is ultimately self-destructive and creates a deeply pessimistic tone in medieval Germanic literature.

5. **Differences Between Modern and Anglo-Saxon Values** *by Fred C. Robinson*   49

The Anglo-Saxon cultural world differs markedly from the modern world in several important respects, including its lack of emphasis on romantic love, its deep concern for public honor and avoidance of shame, the centrality of gift giving in sustaining political loyalty, and its deep respect for the inscrutable workings of fate.

Chapter 2: The Heroic Character of Beowulf

H   1. **The Conflicting Demands of Heroic Strength and Kingly Wisdom**
by John Leyerle   56

There is an inherent conflict between the Anglo-Saxon expectations of a hero and a king. The hero is expected to act to achieve individual glory; the king is expected to act for the good of his people. Beowulf attempts but fails to fulfill both roles.

2. **The Corruption of Beowulf**
by Margaret E. Goldsmith   63

Beowulf's decision to fight the dragon alone at the end of the story need not be seen as bad. But coupled with Beowulf's bold attitude is an excessive concern for the treasure hoard and for the glory of achieving such a treasure. In losing to the dragon because of his concern for earthly possessions, he reenacts the fall of mankind.

H   3. **Beowulf's Heroic Death**
by J.D.A. Ogilvy and Donald C. Baker   69

Beowulf embodies a valiant stoicism in difficult circumstances. His death is not due to excessive pride, nor is it meaningless, as some have claimed; rather, the poem simply reminds us that even the greatest heroes are mortal.

4. **The Heroic Standards of Beowulf's World**
by Michael Swanton   74

Beowulf embodies a unique and powerful version of heroism, one able to take on the most mysterious and evil forces that threaten society. Beowulf is a tragic hero, though he does not suffer from a classical "tragic flaw" or from excessive pride. Rather, he is a model king for his society, though his heroic acts are themselves subject to time and fate.

H   5. **The Failure of the Heroic Ideal** *by Bernard F. Huppé*   82

Christian and heroic ideals and values are both present in *Beowulf* and seem to be in frequent conflict; one explanation for this is that the world depicted in the poem is pagan, while the perspective of the poet is Christian. This insight leads to the conclusion that Beowulf's ideals and values are empty and flawed, and that his death represents the futility of heroic aspirations for glory and fame.

6. The Fatal Contradiction in *Beowulf*
   by John D. Niles   89
   Beowulf is a selfless, responsible, and admirable hero who
   does not suffer from a tragic flaw as many previous critics
   have argued. There is no fatal contradiction of values in the
   poem; rather Beowulf fulfills the heroic code and the re-
   sponsibilities of kingship in all respects.

Chapter 3: Thematic and Structural Issues in *Beowulf*

1. The Struggle Between Order and Chaos
   in *Beowulf* by John Halverson   99
   The world of *Beowulf* is one of fragile stability, with chaos
   lurking just outside the shadows of civilization. The mead
   hall symbolizes all that is good in human society—fellow-
   ship, joy, harmony, and order—yet that society is constantly
   under threat from forces of nature and of evil. The poem
   leads us to the conclusion that reliance on individual heroism for the stability of society, rather than secure institutions, is a recipe for disaster.

2. Grendel's Mother and the Women of *Beowulf*
   by Jane Chance   107
   How should the women in *Beowulf* be interpreted? Do they
   play significant roles in their society or are they merely
   passive sufferers, their fate controlled entirely by men?
   Though passive suffering is the lot of the human women in
   the poem, Grendel's mother provides a challenge to that
   passivity in the way she undertakes an active revenge for
   the death of her son.

3. The Finn Episode and Revenge in *Beowulf*
   by Martin Camargo   112
   The Finn Episode is the longest digression in *Beowulf*, a
   grim depiction of treachery and bloody revenge that serves
   as a sour commentary on the revenge ethic throughout the
   poem. The suffering of the main female character, Hildeburh, is shared by all the poem's women, whose peace-
   bringing role is constantly shattered by the male obsession
   with revenge.

4. Treachery and Betrayal in *Beowulf*
   by Hugh Magennis   120
   Beowulf depicts a world in which order and stability are dependent on loyalty to leaders, yet it is also a world in which
   genuine loyalty is more often the exception than the rule.
   Unlike so many others, Beowulf is the one character in the
   poem who exemplifies loyalty as an unselfish faithfulness.
   Even Beowulf's followers fail him in this regard.

5. The Digressions in *Beowulf* by David Wright   125

The numerous digressions in *Beowulf* are far from arbitrary
interruptions, as some early readers of the poem thought.
Rather, the digressions and allusions, which are obscure to
us, contain stories familiar to *Beowulf*'s Anglo-Saxon audiences. Further, these stories frequently serve as commentary on the main action of the poem, creating an atmosphere of impending doom around Beowulf and his heroics.

Chronology   129

For Further Research   131

Index   134

FOREWORD

*"'Tis the good reader that
makes the good book."*

Ralph Waldo Emerson

The story's bare facts are simple: The captain, an old and scarred seafarer, walks with a peg leg made of whale ivory. He relentlessly drives his crew to hunt the world's oceans for the great white whale that crippled him. After a long search, the ship encounters the whale and a fierce battle ensues. Finally the captain drives his harpoon into the whale, but the harpoon line catches the captain about the neck and drags him to his death.

A simple story, a straightforward plot—yet, since the 1851 publication of Herman Melville's *Moby-Dick*, readers and critics have found many meanings in the struggle between Captain Ahab and the whale. To some, the novel is a cautionary tale that depicts how Ahab's obsession with revenge leads to his insanity and death. Others believe that the whale represents the unknowable secrets of the universe and that Ahab is a tragic hero who dares to challenge fate by attempting to discover this knowledge. Perhaps Melville intended Ahab as a criticism of Americans' tendency to become involved in well-intentioned but irrational causes. Or did Melville model Ahab after himself, letting his fictional character express his anger at what he perceived as a cruel and distant god?

Although literary critics disagree over the meaning of *Moby-Dick*, readers do not need to choose one particular interpretation in order to gain an understanding of Melville's novel. Instead, by examining various analyses, they can gain numerous insights into the issues that lie under the surface of the basic plot. Studying the writings of literary critics can also aid readers in making their own assessments of *Moby-Dick* and other literary works and in developing analytical thinking skills.

The Greenhaven Literary Companion Series was created with these goals in mind. Designed for young adults, this unique anthology series provides an engaging and comprehensive introduction to literary analysis and criticism. The essays included in the Literary Companion Series are chosen for their accessibility to a young adult audience and are expertly edited in consideration of both the reading and comprehension levels of this audience. In addition, each essay is introduced by a concise summation that presents the contributing writer's main themes and insights. Every anthology in the Literary Companion Series contains a varied selection of critical essays that cover a wide time span and express diverse views. Wherever possible, primary sources are represented through excerpts from authors' notebooks, letters, and journals and through contemporary criticism.

Each title in the Literary Companion Series pays careful consideration to the historical context of the particular author or literary work. In-depth biographies and detailed chronologies reveal important aspects of authors' lives and emphasize the historical events and social milieu that influenced their writings. To facilitate further research, every anthology includes primary and secondary source bibliographies of articles and/or books selected for their suitability for young adults. These engaging features make the Greenhaven Literary Companion series ideal for introducing students to literary analysis in the classroom or as a library resource for young adults researching the world's great authors and literature.

Exceptional in its focus on young adults, the Greenhaven Literary Companion Series strives to present literary criticism in a compelling and accessible format. Every title in the series is intended to spark readers' interest in leading American and world authors, to help them broaden their understanding of literature, and to encourage them to formulate their own analyses of the literary works that they read. It is the editors' hope that young adult readers will find these anthologies to be true companions in their study of literature.

INTRODUCTION

A brief perusal of the first few pages of *Beowulf* reveals a mysterious world. A funeral ship full of treasure is set adrift on the open sea, a grim manlike monster that haunts the wastelands attacks a feasting hall and eats its inhabitants. It is a strange, distant text, unlike anything most modern readers have read before. And yet this strange story of a hero who kills monsters and rescues societies has a charm and relevance that can surprise and enchant modern readers, especially if given some knowledge of the world the poem reveals to us. Providing that perspective is one of the primary goals of this volume.

The readings collected in this Greenhaven Literary Companion are accessible to first-time readers of *Beowulf*, readers without a background in medieval history or the heroic literary tradition. The selections address the issues and concerns that arise in class discussion among first-time readers of the poem in translation. With this principle of accessibility in mind, a number of well-known scholars and advanced essays were necessarily excluded. The essays in this collection, written by *Beowulf* scholars at universities and colleges in the United States and England, have been selected primarily for their ability to illuminate a particular facet of *Beowulf* or the society from which it emerged.

In the class approaching *Beowulf* for the first time, there is seldom time for discussion of such scholarly concerns as the dating of the poem, its relation to the oral-formulaic tradition of poetry, the rhythm of the poem (especially if a prose translation is used), and literary and historical sources and analogues. On the other hand, such issues as the bond of loyalty among Beowulf's troop of men, the nature of Beowulf's heroism, the poem's attitude toward the revenge code, and the function of the poem's many digressions confront all first-time readers. These concerns have been organized into three sections addressing the traditional literary concepts of background, character, and theme and plot.

Whether read individually or together, the essays in this volume can provide a useful introduction to the issues and problems that commonly puzzle first-time readers. They may also be useful in stimulating discussion and focusing written analysis of the Old English poem *Beowulf.*

THE *BEOWULF* POET AND HIS WORLD

There is no doubt that *Beowulf* is a strange poem of a strange society, with a drinking hall at its center, a hero known for his tremendous swimming and his incredible hand grip, and monsters lurking about on the misty moors. *Beowulf* is a window into a dimly lit, distant, and mysterious world; yet it is a world strongly linked to ours through shared values and a shared language. For even after the passage of many hundreds of years, we are still essentially speaking the language spoken by the characters in *Beowulf. Mother, hand, life, man, house, old, sword, land, world,* and *wonder* are just a few of the words found in *Beowulf* that are still in use, though in the original, untranslated poem they appear as *moder, hond, lif, man, hus, eald, swearde, londe, worulde,* and *wundor.* Over 80 percent of the words we use in everyday speech come directly from Old English. Since the recovery of *Beowulf* from the shelves of a scholar's library, this poem has fascinated modern readers with its depiction of our linguistic ancestors. What kind of people were they? How much are we still like them? Apart from all our technological advances, what basic human concerns do we share with the inhabitants of *Beowulf*?

Beowulf is the oldest English-language text that most readers will ever encounter. As *Beowulf* scholar Michael Swanton observes:

> *Beowulf* is to English what the *Odyssey* and the *Iliad* are to Greek language and literature. The oldest piece of vernacular literature of any substance not only in England but the whole of Europe, it breathes the true spirit of the northern Heroic Age.[1]

As many of the writers in this volume point out, much remains unknown about the writer of *Beowulf.* Most scholars agree that this is a good part of the challenge and the fun of

1. Michael Swanton, Beowulf: *Edited with an Introduction, Notes, and New Prose Translation.* Manchester: Manchester University Press, 1978, p. 1.

interpreting *Beowulf,* which remains a bit of a mystery even for advanced readers.

THE SURVIVAL OF THE POEM

While it may not qualify as a mystery in itself, how the one extant copy of the poem survived is a fascinating story in its own right. One handwritten copy of *Beowulf* exists in the British Museum in London. Scholars have dated the copy at about A.D. 1000, about five hundred years before the widespread use of the printing press. It was hand copied probably by a monk in a monastery. The surviving copy of *Beowulf* is known to be the product of two copyists, but nothing is known about the text these men were recopying, which may have been many times removed from the original source of the poem.

The poem was undoubtedly preserved for hundreds of years in a monastery. Then, in the early sixteenth century, when the Church of England converted from Catholicism to Protestantism, King Henry VIII ordered the dissolution of the monasteries, and much of their contents, including many books, was destroyed. The single copy of *Beowulf* that somehow survived surfaced in the hands of a private collector, Lawrence Nowell, who mentions it in 1563. The work next seems to have come into the possession of the scholar and antiquarian Sir Robert Cotton, where it was bound in a volume catalogued as Cotton Vitellius A15. Slightly damaged by a fire in 1731, *Beowulf* eventually made its way into the British Museum.

THE *BEOWULF* POET

The first real mystery about *Beowulf* is that next to nothing is known about the poem's author. What is known comes from applying deductive reasoning to evidence found in the poem itself. For example, consistency of style suggests that the poem was written by one person rather than by several poets reworking the poem over the years. Also, the use of several conventional poetic devices suggests an educated person. The presence of certain repeated phrases and formula words suggests that the poem may well have been originally produced and disseminated by memory (the oral tradition) before our poet undertook to put the story on paper. Further, the clear references to God and to the story of Cain and Abel from the Bible strongly suggest that the poet was a Christian rather than a pagan.

Apart from these reasonable inferences, little else can be said with certainty. By studying the dialects of Anglo-Saxon in the surviving copy, scholars have tried to locate the poem's place of origin, but no clear consensus has emerged on this issue. The dating of the poem is similarly difficult; according to the leading scholars, the poet could have composed *Beowulf* anytime from A.D. 700 to 950. The *Beowulf* poet's familiarity with the range of Germanic legends mentioned in the work suggests that he may well have been a *scop;* that is, one who sang stories of these legendary ancestors in the court setting to entertain the aristocracy. But this too is conjecture.

Scholars agree that the *Beowulf* poet was Christian, yet he chose to write the story of a Geatish hero from central Sweden, living in pre-Christian times, whose adventures are set in Denmark and Sweden. *Beowulf* scholar Michael Swanton provides one explanation for this choice:

> The early English minstrel derived his topics from almost any part of Germanic Europe. His heroes may have been Burgundians, Goths, Franks, or men of a host of lesser known tribes. . . . Most of the historical characters referred to in *Beowulf* are well-known figures from Migration times when the Germanic tribes of Northern Europe began their great journeys south and west, land-taking, forming new kingdoms out of what had been the Roman Empire, and laying the foundations for medieval and modern Europe. The Anglo-Saxons recognized themselves part of this movement, and long preserved detailed traditions respecting their origins—much as European immigrants to modern America preserve quite precise oral information as to their antecedents.[2]

Thus, the *Beowulf* poet's choice of story may have originated from respect for his ancestors and those of his audience.

THE WORLD OF *BEOWULF*

The world portrayed in *Beowulf* is one of remarkable instability, reflecting the tentative, transitory nature of early medieval tribal societies in northern Europe. The society of the *Beowulf* poet was forged out of invasions and warfare between tribes, and early audiences of the poem would have understood the difficult challenges entailed in maintaining civilization in a hostile world. The England of the *Beowulf* poet began to take shape around A.D. 400. After almost four hundred years of occupation, Roman troops withdrew from England as the Roman Empire began to collapse due to the invasions of Germanic tribes from eastern Europe. After the Romans withdrew from England, Northern Germanic groups—notably the Angles, Saxons, and the Jutes—began to invade and settle Britain themselves, conquering the Romanized Celtic inhabitants of Britain

2. Swanton, *Beowulf*, pp. 6–7.

in the early 500s. The Angle and Saxon (Anglo-Saxon) culture and language that evolved out of this conquest held sway in southern England in the form of numerous small kingdoms for nearly six hundred years, though the eighth and ninth centuries were marked by countless raids from and two major wars with the Vikings from Scandinavia. These Vikings succeeded in conquering most of the English kingdoms of the time (leaving only the kingdom of the West Saxons intact), and they settled the northeastern portion of England as their own. Many Anglo-Saxons lived with the persistent fear that one's kingdom or tribe could be swallowed up or destroyed at any time.

The societies depicted in *Beowulf* reflect similar anxieties about the impermanence and instability of tribal society. The mighty hall Heorot, which Beowulf rescues early in the poem, is destroyed by war by the poem's end, and King Hrothgar and his Danish people are scattered. After Beowulf becomes king of the Geats and rules for fifty years, his own hall is destroyed and his people scattered as well. The transitory nature of these societies seems to be historically accurate; historical records prove the existence of the Geats, for example, but their demise remains a mystery. The disappearance of the Geats is a fate the *Beowulf* poet may well have feared for his own people, for, during the two centuries of the poem's probable composition, England was subjected to the frequent invasions and depredations of the Vikings.

THE VALUES OF WARFARE

The cultural values of the *Beowulf* poet are essentially Anglo-Saxon, placing an importance on the warrior and heroic values. The deeds of war are the preeminent subject matter of poem and song in the society depicted in *Beowulf,* and the values of warfare were paramount to the poem's first audiences as well. As *Beowulf* scholars J.D.A. Ogilvy and Donald C. Baker have observed:

> It is very difficult for modern readers to recapture the Anglo-Saxon attitude toward war as the natural occupation of the gentleman. . . . To such men war was something between a sport and a religion: a way to profit, a path to glory—almost a moral obligation.[3]

Beowulf shows us a society organized around a leader, usually a king, who maintains a troop of warriors, the *comitatus*, whose loyalty to their leader is the unifying principle of the society. Warfare between one's tribe and neighboring

3. J.D.A. Ogilvy and Donald C. Baker, *Reading* Beowulf: *An Introduction to the Poem, Its Background, and Its Style.* Norman: University of Oklahoma Press, 1983, p. 103.

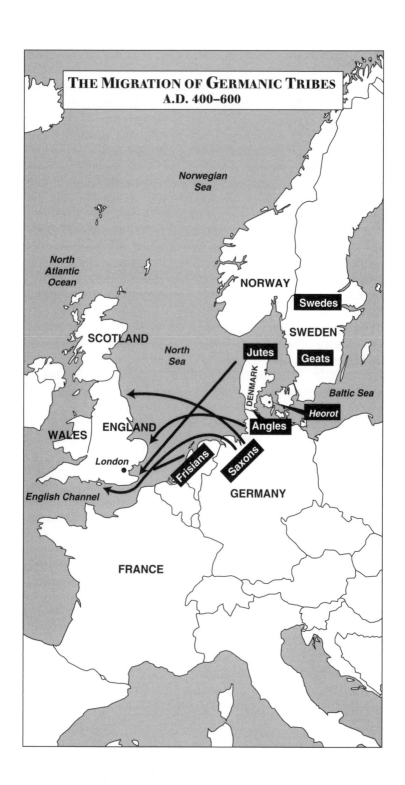

THE MIGRATION OF GERMANIC TRIBES
A.D. 400–600

Norwegian
Sea

North
Atlantic
Ocean

NORWAY

Swedes

SCOTLAND

SWEDEN

Geats

North
Sea

Jutes

DENMARK

Baltic Sea

Heorot

ENGLAND

Angles

WALES

London

Frisians

Saxons

English Channel

GERMANY

FRANCE

tribes was common, and the distribution of the spoils of war by the king to his followers was itself one of the most important social acts unifying the society by cementing loyalty. The values of combat, courage, and tenacity in fighting for one's king were the most admired virtues in this society. Warfare between tribes, however, is not the central conflict of the poem. For the *Beowulf* poet, battles with mysterious monsters are more fascinating than battles between tribes.

While a number of the tribes and stories identified in *Beowulf* can be historically verified in Scandinavian records, only one date can be established with relative certainty, and that is the raid on the Netherlands by King Hygelac in about 521, which resulted in Hygelac's death. According to the poem, Beowulf himself participated in and survived this raid. Scholars agree that the *Beowulf* poet was putting his story on paper around two to three hundred years after this historical event. Perhaps the most significant event taking place in this historical gap is the conversion of Anglo-Saxon society to Christianity, a process that began in earnest in about A.D. 597. This yawning gap between the *Beowulf* poet and his subject matter, along with the intervention of Christian values and perspective, has raised many questions about how the poet wants his audience to understand Beowulf and his pre-Christian, warlike brand of heroism.

A FUSION OF CHRISTIAN AND PAGAN VALUES

One dilemma that has engaged *Beowulf* scholars in recent years is the potential clash of values of a Christian poet telling the story of a pagan hero. Does the poet admire Beowulf's heroism or condemn it? As with many aspects of *Beowulf,* there are competing attitudes on this point. One view holds that the poet clearly admires the hero in spite of his pagan beliefs. As noted scholar Fred C. Robinson has argued:

> A combined admiration and regret is the dominant tone in *Beowulf* and one of the poet's signal triumphs was to adopt the precisely appropriate style for striking that tone. Admiration for pagans, however, has often been judged a highly improbable attitude for medieval Christians to assume. Many readers have held that a moral revulsion is the only possible reaction that a converted Anglo-Saxon could have when confronted with pagans. But . . . this is not the case.[4]

4. Fred C. Robinson, Beowulf *and the Appositive Style.* Knoxville: University of Tennessee Press, 1985, pp. 11–12.

Various historical writings by Christians reveal a tone of compassion and tolerance toward the Anglo-Saxon culture they were in the process of converting. And scholars have shown that Anglo-Saxon values were not eradicated after conversion to Christianity; many, including the revenge ethic, continued to coexist with Christian values for many years. In this view, the poet is simply telling the story of an heroic ancestor; any criticism would be out of place.

Other well-known *Beowulf* scholars differ with this perspective, claiming that the tone condemns Beowulf and his society. This view frequently holds that the poem is subtly ironic and that it is ultimately critical, rather than admiring, of the false values and destructive tendencies depicted in *Beowulf.* As Bernard F. Huppé puts it:

> This hypothesis assumes that the fictional world of *Beowulf* is pagan, its point of view Christian. From the Christian point of view, the pagan events of the poem reveal the limits of heathen society, the limits of the righteous pagan, and the limits of the heroic ideal.[5]

From this viewpoint, Beowulf is only heroic in a shallow way since he lives in a society that lacks Christian values and perspectives.

Yet a third viewpoint claims to find admiration of Beowulf himself in the poem, but condemnation of the values of his society. As Margaret E. Goldsmith argues:

> The description of Beowulf's passing is designed both to celebrate the valour and nobility of a great hero of the past and to look with compassion upon the limited horizons and misdirected aims of the unregenerate sons of Adam.[6]

BEOWULF AS A HERO

For many readers of *Beowulf* the behavior of the hero is problematic, especially at the end of the poem. Whether the *Beowulf* poet wants the reader to admire the hero or see him as flawed or even as a failure is left ambiguous. All three interpretations have been argued by twentieth-century scholars, and it may be the case that the *Beowulf* poet intended to raise these questions without providing easy answers. As scholar Howell D. Chickering Jr. observes, "Whether Beowulf is an ideal king or flawed by his heroic quest for fame remains a question that disturbs every full interpretation of the poem's philosophy."[7]

5. Bernard F. Huppé, *The Hero in the Earthly City: A Reading of* Beowulf. Binghamton: State University of New York Press, 1984, p. 36. 6. Margaret E. Goldsmith, *The Mode and Meaning of* Beowulf. London: Athlone, 1970, p. 241. 7. Howell D. Chickering Jr., Beowulf: *A Dual-Language Edition.* 2nd ed. Garden City; NY: Anchor-Doubleday, 1982, p. 269.

One benchmark for understanding Beowulf's heroic behavior is to examine his enemies. The reader should question, for example, whether the poem's three monsters are representations of a biblical evil or symbolic of the ancient forces of nature and whether there are significant differences between the first two monsters and the dragon at the end. The monsters are essential for judging Beowulf's heroism since he never fights a human opponent. Yet they are presented in a deliberately ambiguous way. Grendel, for example, is hardly described at all, leaving the reader free to imagine all manner of horrible creature. As scholar John D. Niles points out:

> When we try to visualize his appearance, each reader is likely to call up a slightly different image. Like his latter-day cousins, Bigfoot, the Yeti, and Sasquatch, Grendel never emerges into the bright light of day. The poet leaves his listeners free to fill out the details of the monster's appearance from the resources of their own imagination.[8]

One fact about Grendel that the poet does give us is that the monster is descended from Cain, the first murderer, the man who killed his own brother in the Book of Genesis in the Bible. These human origins, coupled with Grendel's size, strength, and cannibalistic tendencies, stir the imagination in a very sinister way.

Whatever the appearance of Grendel and his mother, though, they clearly represent something antithetical to civilization. Grendel's initial attacks are motivated by his resentment of the joy and music he hears coming from the great hall Heorot. Their evil force poses a threat to the fragile society of Heorot, which, for that time, represents European civilization at its best. The dragon that appears late in the poem is also a rather ambiguous creature. It is clearly destructive, antagonistic, an almost instinctual force, and it seems intent on the annihilation of Beowulf's society. But whether we see these monsters as purely evil or as more representative of forces of untamed nature, they serve to show Beowulf in his heroic role of defender of civilization.

BEOWULF'S CONCEPTION OF HIMSELF

In this respect, some scholars have argued that Beowulf's heroism changes by the end of the poem. While, for example, he is completely admirable and heroic in his defeat of Grendel and his mother, his encounter with the dragon reveals character flaws: He forgets the responsible goal of protector for the short-

8. John D. Niles, Beowulf: *The Poem and Its Tradition.* Cambridge, MA: Harvard University Press, 1983, p. 8.

term goal of glory. John Leyerle argues that Beowulf's combined roles of king and hero are inherently in conflict.

> An individual's desire for glory . . . becomes an increasingly
> dangerous motivation as a man's responsibility for leadership
> grows. Even without such a desire, a leader's excessive re-
> liance on his personal strength easily brings calamity.[9]

Some scholars argue that Beowulf's defeat by the dragon
at the end, and the subsequent demise of the Geats, who
could not survive without the strong leadership of Beowulf,
is an implicit condemnation of Beowulf. The poet is making
the case that Beowulf suffers from a tragic flaw, such as am-
bition for fame and glory, or valuing earthly things like gold
or fame above spiritual things. Scholar Margaret E. Goldsmith, for example, finds him to be "blinded by arrogance
and desire for the treasure"[10] at the end.

Other critics of the poem criticize these conclusions, arguing
that the author clearly intends to praise its hero at the beginning and the end. As British scholar Bruce Mitchell has put it:

> The fact that Beowulf dies is no reason for believing that he has
> been deserted by God or that he has done something wrong. That
> sinners live and saints die is a fact of everyday experience which
> does not prove that God is with the former and against the lat-
> ter. . . . The poem does not read to me like a criticism of Be-
> owulf. . . . We need to remember that Beowulf was not immortal
> and that the misery which followed his death is no reason for
> blaming Beowulf, but is merely part of the machinery of life.[11]

Here again, all the evidence the reader needs concerning
Beowulf's heroic stature is contained in the poem, but the doors
of interpretation are wide open. Readers who are amazed at Beowulf's heroic exploits in the first half of the poem are drawn to
participate in Beowulf's moral choices at the end. Though Beowulf may not examine his own motives or see the ramifications
of his choices, he acts according to what he does know, the
heroic value system that has given his life meaning. Though Beowulf may not be able to rationally articulate his behavior, modern readers can appreciate a hero who puts his life on the line,
without hesitation, when awesome and destructive forces
threaten his society. And perhaps, in the end, the lack of a single
unifying interpretation of Beowulf's character is part of the
poem's long-lasting appeal and its challenge. Although our
dragons are not Beowulf's, the question remains, When we
are "confronted by the dragon," how will we respond?

9. John Leyerle, "Beowulf the Hero and the King," *Medium Aevum* 34 (1965): p. 97.
10. Goldsmith, *The Mode and Meaning of* Beowulf, p. 228. 11. Bruce Mitchell, *Beowulf.*
Trans. Kevin Crossley-Holland. London: Farrar, Straus & Giroux, 1968, pp. 18–19.

CHAPTER 1

Social and Cultural Context

Beowulf as a Heroic-Elegiac Poem

J.R.R. Tolkien

British scholar J.R.R. Tolkien is best known to Americans as the author of *The Hobbit* and *The Lord of the Rings* trilogy. But for nearly thirty years, he was also a professor of medieval literature at Oxford University. The following selection was first delivered as a lecture in 1936. Prior to this very influential essay, critics tended to compare *Beowulf* unfavorably with the great classical epic poems the *Odyssey,* the *Iliad,* and the *Aeneid.* Tolkien contends that it is unfair to hold *Beowulf* to classical standards since *Beowulf* is more a heroic-elegiac poem than an epic poem. Tolkien defines heroic-elegiac as a celebration of the accomplishments of a great hero, conveyed with a tone of mournfulness and loss. Tolkien also argues that the poem has a more balanced structure than earlier critics have allowed.

In *Beowulf* we have an historical poem about the pagan past, or an attempt at one—literal historical fidelity founded on modern research was, of course, not attempted. It is a poem by a learned man writing of old times, who looking back on the heroism and sorrow feels in them something permanent and something symbolical. So far from being a confused semi-pagan—historically unlikely for a man of this sort in the period—he brought probably *first* to his task a knowledge of Christian poetry, especially that of the Cædmon school, and especially *Genesis.* He makes his minstrel sing in Heorot of the Creation of the earth and the lights of Heaven. So excellent is this choice as the theme of the harp that maddened Grendel lurking joyless in the dark without that it matters little whether this is anachronistic or not. *Secondly,* to his task the poet brought a considerable learning in native lays and traditions: only by learning and training could such things be acquired, they were no more born naturally into an Englishman of the seventh or eighth centuries, by simple virtue of being an 'Anglo-Saxon', than ready-made knowledge of poetry and history is inherited at birth by modern children.

It would seem that, in his attempt to depict ancient pre-Christian days, intending to emphasize their nobility, and the desire of the good for truth, he turned naturally when delineating the great King of Heorot to the Old Testament. In the *folces hyrde* [people's keeper, i.e., king] of the Danes we have much of the shepherd patriarchs and kings of Israel, servants of the one God, who attribute to His mercy all the good things that come to them in this life. We have in fact a Christian English conception of the noble chief before Christianity, who could lapse (as could Israel) in times of temptation into idolatry. On the other hand, the traditional matter in English, not to mention the living survival of the heroic code and temper among the noble households of ancient England, enabled him to draw differently, and in some respects much closer to the actual heathen *hæloth* [hero], the character of Beowulf, especially as a young knight, who used his great gift of *mægen* [prowess] to earn *dom* [glory] and *lof* [fame] among men and posterity.

Beowulf is not an actual picture of historic Denmark or Geatland or Sweden about A.D. 500. But it is (if with certain minor defects) on a general view a self-consistent picture, a construction bearing clearly the marks of design and thought. The whole must have succeeded admirably in creating in the minds of the poet's contemporaries the illusion of surveying a past, pagan but noble and fraught with a deep significance—a past that itself had depth and reached backward into a dark antiquity of sorrow. This impression of depth is an effect and a justification of the use of episodes and allusions to old tales, mostly darker, more pagan, and desperate than the foreground. . . .

The criticism that the important matters are put on the outer edges misses this point of artistry, and indeed fails to see why the old things have in *Beowulf* such an appeal: it is the poet himself who made antiquity so appealing. His poem has more value in consequence, and is a greater contribution to early mediaeval thought than the harsh and intolerant view that consigned all the heroes to the devil. We may be thankful that the product of so noble a temper has been preserved by chance (if such it be) from the dragon of destruction.

THE POEM'S STRUCTURE

The general structure of the poem, so viewed, is not really difficult to perceive, if we look to the main points, the strategy, and neglect the many points of minor tactics. We must dismiss, of course, from mind the notion that *Beowulf* is a 'narrative poem', that it tells a tale or intends to tell a tale sequentially.... The poem was not meant to advance, steadily or unsteadily. It is essentially a balance, an opposition of ends and beginnings. In its simplest terms it is a contrasted description of two moments in a great life, rising and setting; an elaboration of the ancient and intensely moving contrast between youth and age, first achievement and final death. It is divided in consequence into two opposed portions, different in matter, manner, and length: A from 1 to 2199 (including an exordium of 52 lines); B from 2200 to 3182 (the end). There is no reason to cavil at this proportion; in any case, for the purpose and the production of the required effect, it proves in practice to be right.

This simple and *static* structure, solid and strong, is in each part much diversified, and capable of enduring this treatment. In the conduct of the presentation of Beowulf's rise to fame on the one hand, and of his kingship and death on the other, criticism can find things to question, especially if it is captious, but also much to praise, if it is attentive. But the only serious weakness, or apparent weakness, is the long recapitulation: the report of Beowulf to Hygelac. This recapitulation is well done. Without serious discrepancy it retells rapidly the events in Heorot, and retouches the account; and it serves to illustrate, since he himself describes his own deeds, yet more vividly the character of a young man, singled out by destiny, as he steps suddenly forth in his full powers. Yet this is perhaps not quite sufficient to justify the repetition. The explanation, if not complete justification, is probably to be sought in different directions.

For one thing, the old tale was not first told or invented by this poet. So much is clear from investigation of the folk-tale analogues. Even the legendary association of the Scylding court with a marauding monster, and with the arrival from abroad of a champion and deliverer was probably already old. The plot was not the poet's; and though he has infused feeling and significance into its crude material, that plot was not a perfect vehicle of the theme or themes that came to hidden life in the poet's mind as he worked upon it. Not an unusual event in literature. For the contrast—youth and death—it would probably have been better, if we had no journeying. If the single nation of the *Geatas* had been the scene, we should have felt the stage not narrower, but symbolically wider. More plainly should we have perceived in one people and their hero all mankind and its heroes. This at any rate I have always myself felt in reading *Beowulf*; but I have also felt that this defect is rectified by the bringing of the tale of Grendel to Geatland. As Beowulf stands in Hygelac's hall and tells his story, he sets his feet firm again in the land of his own people, and is no longer in danger of appearing a mere *wrecca*, an errant adventurer and slayer of bogies that do not concern him.

There is in fact a double division in the poem: the fundamental one already referred to, and a secondary but important division at line 1887. After that the essentials of the previous part are taken up and compacted, so that all the tragedy of Beowulf is contained between 1888 and the end. But, of course, without the first half we should miss much incidental illustration; we should miss also the dark background of the court of Heorot that loomed as large in glory and doom in ancient northern imagination as the court of Arthur: no vision of the past was complete without it. And (most important) we should lose the direct contrast of youth and age in the persons of Beowulf and Hrothgar which is one of the chief purposes of this section: it ends with the pregnant words *oth thæt hine yldo benam mægenes wynnum, se the oft manegum scod* [until that he was deprived of the joys of strength by old age, which has often harmed many].

NOT A ROMANTIC TALE

In any case we must not view this poem as in intention an exciting narrative or a romantic tale. The very nature of Old English metre is often misjudged. In it there is no single rhythmic pattern progressing from the beginning of a line to the end, and repeated with variation in other lines. The lines do not go according to a tune. They are founded on a balance; an opposition between two halves of roughly equivalent phonetic weight, and significant content, which are more often rhythmically contrasted than similar. They are more like masonry than music. In this fundamental fact of poetic expression I think there is a parallel to the total structure of *Beowulf. Beowulf* is indeed the most successful Old English poem because in it the elements, language, metre, theme, structure, are all most nearly in harmony. Judgement of the verse has often gone astray through listening for an accentual rhythm and pattern: and it seems to halt and stumble. Judgement of the theme goes astray through considering it as the narrative handling of a plot: and it seems to halt and stumble. Language and verse, of course, differ from stone or wood or paint, and can be only heard or read in a time-sequence; so that in any poem that deals at all with characters and events some narrative element must be present. We have none the less in *Beowulf* a method and structure that within the limits of the verse-kind approaches rather to sculpture or painting. It is a composition not a tune.

This is clear in the second half. In the struggle with Grendel one can as a reader dismiss the certainty of literary experience that the hero will not in fact perish, and allow oneself to share the hopes and fears of the Geats upon the shore. In the second part the author has no desire whatever that the issue should remain open, even according to literary convention. There is no need to hasten like the messenger, who rode to bear the lamentable news to the waiting people (2892 ff.). They may have hoped, but we are not supposed to. By now we are supposed to have grasped the plan. Disaster is foreboded. Defeat is the theme. Triumph over the foes of man's precarious fortress is over, and we approach slowly and reluctantly the inevitable victory of death. . . .

In structure . . . [*Beowulf*] is curiously strong, in a sense inevitable, though there are defects of detail. The general design of the poet is not only defensible, it is, I think, admirable. There may have previously existed stirring verse dealing in straightforward manner and even in natural sequence with Beowulf's deeds, or with the fall of Hygelac; or again with the fluctuations of the feud between the houses of Hrethel the Geat and Ongentheow the Swede; or with the tragedy of the Heathobards, and the treason that destroyed the Scylding dynasty. Indeed this must be admitted to be practically certain: it was the existence of such connected legends connected in the mind, not necessarily dealt with in chronicle fashion or in long semi-historical poems—

that permitted the peculiar use of them in *Beowulf.* This poem cannot be criticized or comprehended, if its original audience is imagined in like case to ourselves, possessing only *Beowulf* in splendid isolation. For *Beowulf* was not designed to tell the tale of Hygelac's fall, or for that matter to give the whole biography of Beowulf, still less to write the history of the Geatish kingdom and its downfall. But it used knowledge of these things for its own purpose to give that sense of perspective, of antiquity with a greater and yet darker antiquity behind. These things are mainly on the outer edges or in the background because they belong there, if they are to function in this way. But in the centre we have an heroic figure of enlarged proportions.

Beowulf is not an 'epic', not even a magnified 'lay'. No terms borrowed from Greek or other literatures exactly fit: there is no reason why they should. Though if we must have a term, we should choose rather 'elegy'. It is an heroic-elegiac poem; and in a sense all its first 3,136 lines are the prelude to a dirge: *him tha gegiredan Geata leode ad ofer eorthan unwaclicne* [then the Geatish people prepared no mean pyre on the earth]: one of the most moving ever written. But for the universal significance which is given to the fortunes of its hero it is an enhancement and not a detraction, in fact it is necessary, that his final foe should be not some Swedish prince, or treacherous friend, but a dragon: a thing made by imagination for just such a purpose. Nowhere does a dragon come in so precisely where he should. But if the hero falls before a dragon, then certainly he should achieve his early glory by vanquishing a foe of similar order.

There is, I think, no criticism more beside the mark than that which some have made, complaining that it is monsters in both halves that is so disgusting; one they could have stomached more easily. That is nonsense. I can see the point of asking for no monsters. I can also see the point of the situation in *Beowulf.* But no point at all in mere reduction of numbers. It would really have been preposterous, if the poet had recounted Beowulf's rise to fame in a 'typical' or 'commonplace' war in Frisia, and then ended him with a dragon. Or if he had told of his cleansing of Heorot, and then brought him to defeat and death in a 'wild' or 'trivial' Swedish invasion! If the dragon is the right end for Beowulf, and I agree with the author that it is, then Grendel is an eminently suitable beginning. They are creatures, *feond mancynnes* [ene-

mies of mankind], of a similar order and kindred significance. Triumph over the lesser and more nearly human is
cancelled by defeat before the older and more elemental.
And the conquest of the ogres comes at the right moment:
not in earliest youth, though the nicors are referred to in
Beowulf's *geogothfeore* [period of youth] as a presage of the
kind of hero we have to deal with; and not during the later
period of recognized ability and prowess; but in that first
moment, which often comes in great lives, when men look
up in surprise and see that a hero has unawares leaped
forth. The placing of the dragon is inevitable: a man can but
die upon his death-day. . . .

And one last point, which those will feel who to-day preserve the ancient *pietas* [reverence] towards the past: *Beowulf*
is not a 'primitive' poem; it is a late one, using the materials
(then still plentiful) preserved from a day already changing
and passing, a time that has now forever vanished, swallowed in oblivion; using them for a new purpose, with a
wider sweep of imagination, if with a less bitter and con-
centrated force. When new *Beowulf* was already antiquarian, in a good sense, and it now produces a singular effect.
For it is now to us itself ancient; and yet its maker was telling
of things already old and weighted with regret, and he
expended his art in making keen that touch upon the heart
which sorrows have that are both poignant and remote. If
the funeral of Beowulf moved once like the echo of an
ancient dirge, far-off and hopeless, it is to us as a memory
brought over the hills, an echo of an echo. There is not much
poetry in the world like this; and though *Beowulf* may not be
among the very greatest poems of our western world and its
tradition, it has its own individual character, and peculiar
solemnity; it would still have power had it been written in
some time or place unknown and without posterity, if it contained no name that could now be recognized or identified
by research. Yet it is in fact written in a language that after
many centuries has still essential kinship with our own, it
was made in this land, and moves in our northern world
beneath our northern sky, and for those who are native to
that tongue and land, it must ever call with a profound
appeal—until the dragon comes.

Anglo-Saxon Language and Traditions in *Beowulf*

Barry Tharaud

In the following essay, *Beowulf* scholar and translator Barry Tharaud explores the dominant culture
established by the Germanic tribes that invaded and
settled Britain. The social obligations and traditions
that bound this civilization together are different
from modern values, and must be understood before
Beowulf can make sense. Tharaud also explicates the
literary and epic principles in the poem.

The original inhabitants of Britain were Celts. In 55 B.C.
Roman legions began to invade Britain, and by A.D. 43
Romans began to establish settlements on the island. For the
next four hundred years Britain was part of the Roman
Empire, until the Romans were forced to withdraw during
the gradual disintegration of the empire. The Germanic
tribes that invaded the Roman Empire (and were in part
responsible for its disintegration) also invaded Britain and
established the dominant culture there. The Middle Ages in
England thus began with the withdrawal of the Romans and
the arrival of various Germanic tribes during the mid–fifth
century, and ended in 1485 with the conclusion of the Wars
of the Roses, the beginning of the revival of learning, and the
beginning of a new political stability—conditions that were
part of a cultural development we now call the Renaissance.

Moreover, the Middle Ages in England can be divided into
the Anglo-Saxon (or Old English) period, and the Norman-
French (or Middle English) period, which began in 1066
with the invasion and conquest of Britain by a Norman duke,
William the Conqueror. There are substantial political, literary, and temperamental differences between the two periods, but by the end of the Middle Ages the foundations of

Reprinted, by permission of the publisher, from *Beowulf,* translated with an introduction by Barry Tharaud, revised edition (Niwot: University Press of Colorado, copyright
1996).

modern English language and culture had been established through a rich mixture of Anglo-Saxon and Norman-French cultures. When we read *Beowulf* and other Old English poems, we encounter the foundations of Anglo-American culture, including ideas and traits of temperament that are still with us today.

EXCELLENCE IN WARFARE

The Anglo-Saxons who began to invade Britain in the fifth century were members of Germanic tribes from what are today the Netherlands, Denmark, northern Germany, and southern Sweden. The invasions occurred over several centuries and were part of a larger movement of northern tribes that eventually overran the Roman Empire. The Germanic tribes shared a common cultural heritage that included closely related languages, customs, and tribal organization, but they apparently lacked the ability or inclination to form a large permanent political confederation—although they were capable of sporadic cooperation during military campaigns. In this respect they were like the Mycenaean Greeks that Homer celebrates in the *Iliad* and *Odyssey;* in fact, readers who are familiar with the heroic ideals expressed in the Homeric epics are already familiar with some of the most important aspects of Anglo-Saxon ideals.

The most important Anglo-Saxon ideal was "excellence"— which ancient Greeks of the heroic and post-heroic ages called *arete.* Although this excellence could be expressed in various ways, it above all was demonstrated by skill and courage and resourcefulness in battle. Ideally, the warrior with the greatest courage would be the king, or "lord," and his courage would be measured by his success in battle and demonstrated by the spoils of war that he and his warriors captured. These spoils were handed over to the lord, who then partially redistributed them to his warriors ("thanes" or "retainers") to reward them according to their courage in battle. Hence such epithets as "ring-giver" and "disperser of treasure" are commonly applied in Anglo-Saxon poetry to the tribal king or lord. The spoils of war thus determined the status of the individual in the warrior band, or *comitatus,* and the comitatus itself was based on the reciprocal loyalty and recognition between thane and lord. These rewards were distributed in the mead hall, which was a symbol of social unity. ("Mead" is a fermented drink.)

THE SPOILS OF WAR AND HEROIC VIRTUE

The spoils of war were not regarded as material wealth as in a modern market economy in which the value of goods and services is determined primarily by the laws of supply and demand. Instead the spoils of war were accounted valuable only as symbols of the courage and resourcefulness that won them. Such spoils would be meaningless in the hands of a person who did not acquire them through valor. For example, when an outlaw steals a gold cup from a dragon's treasure hoard in Part Three of *Beowulf,* it is not only an act of theft: It is also a blow against the entire heroic system because it reduces the symbolic value of things to mere material value. It is a fall from the heroic world to a less ideal world in which symbols are deceptive and equivocal: Material objects no longer accurately represent ideals but are merely "things." It is appropriate therefore that the wealth of the dragon's hoard is not distributed at the end of the epic: First because Beowulf the "ring-giver" is dead; and secondly because all but one of his thanes deserted him in his time of need and therefore the treasure cannot symbolize the excellence of these men: They have failed to fulfill their vows and obligations to their lord, and therefore the spoils of battle from the dragon's hoard are symbolically meaningless.

We can see then that the heroic society depicted in *Beowulf* and in Anglo-Saxon poetry generally is based upon a system of ideals that includes courage, strength, and loyalty, which are then symbolically expressed through material objects (battle spoils). But such is the nature of all societies, and hence it seems fair to enquire what symbols and ideals form the foundation of one's own society, and to ask how worthy such ideals appear when they are compared with the Anglo-Saxon ideals of *Beowulf.*

One can also go a step further in the examination of Anglo-Saxon ideals: Battle spoils embody heroic virtues such as courage and skill, but heroic excellence is itself a divine spark within man. Hence it is not surprising that Beowulf is superhuman or semi-divine, since he possesses such a great capacity for divine excellence. And because immortality is an attribute of divinity, the hero who expresses such divine excellence in actions is worthy to be immortalized by the song of the poet ("bard " or "scop") who preserves the fame of the hero in a society where writing does not exist.

FEATURES OF ANGLO-SAXON POETRY

The Anglo-Saxon bard's poetry, which confers immortality on the hero, is both stylistically and linguistically different from modern English poetry. In fact, Old English is a different language from modern English, and so when we read the poem in English, we are reading a translation from a "dead" language that is no longer spoken. . . .

Anglo-Saxon poetry generally does not use rhyme as a principle of structural organization. Instead, it uses a system of alliteration, whereby stressed syllables beginning with the same sound are linked together. Each line is divided by a pause, or "caesura," and there are two stressed syllables in each half-line. At least one of the two stressed syllables in the first half of the line must alliterate with the first stress in the second half of the line, and stressed vowels are considered to alliterate with each other. . . .

Another technique that distinguishes Anglo-Saxon poetry is the use of compound metaphor, or "kenning," whereby the sea is called the "whale's road" or the "swan's path.". . .

Alliteration, which is the main principle of organization in Old English verse, gives Anglo-Saxon poetry a characteristic forcefulness that seems to be a reflection of the Saxon temperament. In the poem *Beowulf* and a number of other Old English poems, the Anglo-Saxon attitudes and values stand out: We are shown glimpses of a life that is harsh and dark and filled with uncertainty—a life in which the principal value is the courage that enables one to face such a world with a grim realism that bears little relation to the romanticized courage expressed by some later poets.

EPIC CONVENTIONS

But the poem does a great deal more than portray a kind of courage. *Beowulf* belongs to a special kind of literature known as epic, which is characterized generally by great length, a dignified tone, and elevated style. An epic tells the story of a people or race during its origins or during some period of crisis. Originally, epics were composed orally—usually in a preliterate culture—and were sung by a bard accompanied by a lyre. This kind of oral epic is sometimes designated "primary epic" by scholars, to distinguish it from the more sophisticated "secondary epic" of literate societies. Primary epic is often anonymous and is not written down until centuries after its composition, while secondary epic is composed to be read rather than sung. Some examples of primary epic are Homer's *Iliad* and *Odyssey*, and the Anglo-Saxon *Beowulf:* examples of secondary epic are Virgil's *Aeneid* and Milton's *Paradise Lost.*

Whether an epic is composed to be sung or to be read, its most important characteristic is that it tells the story of a society or culture—usually during a time of crisis—in such a way as to expose contradictions inherent in the values of that society. For example, the contradiction often centers around the conflict between the individual and society. In *Beowulf,* the pre-English Anglo-Saxon culture exists in a climate of violence and uncertainty: The central events of the poem are the depredations of Grendel, Grendel's mother, and the fire dragon—violent cataclysms that threaten the very existence of society.

Moreover, throughout the poem we are given flashbacks of previous violence and chaos, and allusions are made to future violence and chaos. Hence the central events of the poem may be more spectacular than normal, but the portrait of a society fighting for its very existence is typical rather than unusual. Under such conditions, the survival of the individual warrior is dependent on a strong social organization that not only protects him but also gives meaning and structure to his life. Furthermore, if the individual is dependent on society for security and a sense of coherence in his life, society is in turn dependent on a strong and skillful leader for *its* survival. . . .

THE SURVIVAL OF SOCIETY

Ideally, the great deeds of the hero affirm *both* the hero and society, and bind them together in a mutually beneficial relationship: Society needs heroic deeds to survive, and the hero needs a social context to give meaning and recognition to his deeds. . . .

The potential conflict between individual and society is suggested in *Beowulf* when Hrothgar warns the hero against the sin of pride. Beowulf successfully slays Grendel and Grendel's mother, and is therefore generously rewarded by King Hrothgar; but Beowulf obviously has the power to take whatever rewards he desires. Instead, he acts for the good of society and subjects himself to Hrothgar's authority. Moreover, when he returns to his homeland, he presents his battle spoils to his lord, Hygelac, and after Hygelac's death he supports the natural succession of Hygelac's son to the throne. Clearly, the outstanding prowess of a hero like Beowulf must be matched by outstanding wisdom and self-mastery, lest he destroy the very society that gives him recognition and humanity. . . .

hero Because Beowulf is heroic both physically and spiritually, he at times seems like the warfaring Christian hero of a later age—and perhaps the poem does reflect some Christian values in addition to pagan heroic values, although scholars disagree about the extent and the nature of the influence. *Beowulf* was probably composed by a single poet sometime between the eighth and tenth centuries, after Britain had been converted to Christianity by missionaries from both Rome and Ireland; but the poem also reflects Anglo-Saxon pagan culture before its conversion to Christianity and before its invasion of Britain. (Although the poem was composed in Christian England, the events take place centuries earlier in the continental homeland of pre-Christian Anglo-Saxons.). . . .

THE FUSION OF VALUES

Anglo-Saxon heroic ideals were apparently so ingrained that when Christianity was *re*-introduced to Britain in the late sixth century (it had previously been introduced in the fourth century by the Romans, who left in the mid–fifth century), Christian and heroic ideals became fused. In Caedmon's poem, "Hymn to the Creation," for example, God is patterned after the Anglo-Saxon lord who rewards his thanes and leads a comitatus: He is described as "Eternal Lord," "Guardian," "Glory-Father," and "Master Almighty," while in another early Anglo-Saxon poem, "The Dream of the Rood," Jesus is described as a strong, stout-hearted young hero, and heaven is a sort of feast in the great mead hall that is paradise.

Although Anglo-Saxon ideals and literary style remained strong and intact to the end of the Old English period, they were rapidly supplanted by new attitudes and literary styles after the Norman invasion of England. The difference between the two periods is immediately apparent when one compares and contrasts Anglo-Saxon with Middle English literature: There are striking differences in style and subject matter, just as in daily life there were striking differences in social and political attitudes between the two periods.

But above all, the most obvious difference between the Old English and Middle English periods is to be found in the language: Old English is a different language from modern English, while Middle English can be easily read and understood, after little or no training, by anyone with a knowledge of modern English. Nevertheless, the Anglo-Saxon influence remains a strong and permanent basis of modern Anglo-American culture. Although the Normans imported a great number of French and Latin words into the English language, Anglo-Saxon is still the backbone of the language: More than sixty percent of the vocabulary in English can be traced back to Latin roots, but of the one thousand most commonly used words in English, some eighty-three percent come from Anglo-Saxon roots. And perhaps Anglo-Saxon moral and cultural influences are as pervasive today in our culture as in our language. The poem *Beowulf,* which embodies Anglo-Saxon culture and language more completely and intensely than any other work of literature, still stands as a great fountainhead of our culture and our language. To understand and appreciate this great epic is to be more intimately acquainted with our culture and ourselves.

Heroic and Social Codes in *Beowulf*

Howell D. Chickering Jr.

The structure and values of Anglo-Saxon society are not obvious to many first-time readers of *Beowulf*. Howell D. Chickering Jr., professor of English at Amherst College, provides valuable background on the Anglo-Saxon culture reflected in *Beowulf*. In the following excerpt from his book *Beowulf: A Dual-Language Edition*, Chickering examines the basic social unit of society—the king and his band of warriors (called a *comitatus*)—feuds within this group, the importance of kinship ties, the status of women, and the nature of kingship.

The Angles, Saxons, and Jutes came to England from the area just below Denmark during the first great wave of Germanic migrations in the fifth century, which also saw the fall of Rome. (The second wave was to be the Viking expansion from Denmark and Norway, to as far south as Sicily, in the ninth and tenth centuries.) These "Engels" (hence "English") brought with them the social pattern of a people on the move, organized principally around individual chieftains and their faithful bands of followers. They were first invited across the Channel, Bede tells us, in A.D. 449 by Vortigern, king of the Britons, to help him repel the Picts and Scots. They found victory so easy and the land so fertile that they moved over in force, subjugating the Britons as well. As they slowly settled into a more stable society, they passed on no legends of their victories in England that we know of, but they preserved memories of heroes from their Continental homeland through an oral poetry now almost wholly lost.

Even more important for classical Old English poetry, they kept alive the ancient Germanic heroic code by which they had lived and died and which made them, in one historian's happy phrase, "an aristocracy of the brave." It is very close to the code described in A.D. 98 by [Roman historian] Tacitus in his *Germania*, a taciturn little treatise that sets barbarian virtue against Roman decadence. The chieftain of the *comitatus*, or small war band, is surrounded by noble warriors, his *comites* 'companions,' who have sworn to defend him with their lives. He, in turn, is unstintingly liberal in giving them gifts and weapons. In Old English, he is their *dryhten* 'lord' and they are his *gedryht* 'troop,' a word with the same root. They are divided into two groups, the *duguth*, or 'doughty' experienced men, and the *geogoth*, or untried 'youths.' Their virtues were those of reckless and absolute personal courage, loyalty to one's chief; and, on the chief's part, generosity and protection. The aim was glory— the fame of "a good name" after death.

In Old English heroic poetry, the chief was often called "the gold-giver," but this lacked the pejorative sense that Tacitus managed to create. Rather, it indicated the Germanic custom of taking the symbolic measure of a man's worth by the amount of gold he could win through valor. Thus the chief, by his large-handed generosity, was asserting his confidence in his man's daring and courage in combats to come; and his follower, by accepting the chief's gift, was vowing an equally perfect fidelity. Tacitus quite rightly emphasized the bloody-minded ferocity behind the *comitatus* oath, but it was still a noble bond between men and not very far from what we now call brotherly love. In Old English religious poetry, it was readily assimilated to the scheme of Christ as the Supreme Chief and the disciples as His *comitatus*. Because of the absolute devotion the "gold-giver" inspired in his followers, this fusion of concepts could be used in religious poetry without the least impropriety. It follows also that if a man was for some reason exiled from his lord and homeland, his resulting misery was irremediable. Under such a code, in such a world, to be exiled was to be without protection by lord or kindred, without friends, means of livelihood, or the respect and trust of others. In the magnificent meditative poems *The Wanderer* and *The Seafarer*, this theme of exile becomes an underlying metaphor that expresses the Christian view of man alone in a desolate world, searching, as St. Paul puts it, for "our heavenly home." In both secular and religious Old English poetry it meant everything to have a lord.

The very first generalization in *Beowulf* sets forth the interdependence in the *comitatus* bond from the leader's point of view:

> So ought a young man,   in his father's household,
> treasure up the future   by his goods and goodness,
> by splendid bestowals,   that later in life
> his chosen men   stand by him in turn,
> his retainers serve him   when war comes.
> By such generosity   any man prospers. (20–25)

The slightly contractual flavor of this maxim is quite in keeping with actual examples from Anglo-Saxon history. When the dragon attacks Beowulf, Wiglaf's impassioned outcry to the cowardly troop illustrates the proper devotion of a retainer. It is anything but "blind loyalty.". . .

FEUDS, REVENGE, AND KINSHIP TIES

Throughout the Anglo-Saxon period, as in some Latin countries today, a man's kin were his strongest support in everyday affairs. If a man was killed, it was the duty of his kinsmen, however remotely related, to avenge him in kind. Naturally, this system led to long-standing, self-propelling vendettas. They might lie dormant for a generation or two and then erupt in a new rash of slayings.

While blood for blood was the most satisfying form of repaying the wrongs done one's kin, an equally respectable and more customary method was a money payment called the *wergild* 'manpayment.' This could be accepted by the kindred of the slain man without loss of face because each man's life had a set money value according to his standing in society. A nobleman or *eorl* was a "man of twelve hundred" shillings (a shilling then being worth vastly more than the modern shilling). The ordinary free man, the *ceorl* (later deteriorating to "churl'), was "a man of two hundred." A slave had no wergild, being only a chattel, and his cost to his owner, usually one pound, was all that had to be paid if he were damaged beyond repair. The Church equated a priest with a noble thane in the scale of wergilds, and a man's monastery assumed the role of his kindred after he took orders. Any compensation would be paid to his monastery. The Church understood, and at times condoned, the unwritten law of blood for blood among the laity, but early it took the position that the wergild was preferable, for practical as well as moral reasons. The scale of payment for priests perhaps reflects the fact that many powerful *œpelingas* 'princes, nobles' entered the Church.

One of the most moving scenes of grief in *Beowulf* is the hero's recollection of the case of King Hrethel, Hygelac's father (2435–70), whose eldest son Herebeald was killed accidentally by an arrow shot by his brother Hæthcyn. Hrethel's unappeasable sorrow lay mainly in the fact that this death had to go unpaid and unavenged, since it had occurred within the kindred. The poet has Beowulf liken it to the sorrow and loss of honor, indeed the loss of any meaning to life, felt by an old *ceorl* when he sees his son hanged as a criminal and can expect no compensation since it is a legal death. Hrethel eventually dies of a broken heart. In both cases, we also see the misery of a father's childlessness in a world where inheritance and patronymics [deriving names from the father's name] figure importantly. The reactions of the old fathers are quite different from the usual responses to such tragedies today and they illustrate the central position of kinship obligations in Anglo-Saxon life.

PEACEFUL HALL AND FAMILY LIFE

Not all was dark in Anglo-Saxon life. The poetry frequently depicts the occupations of the happy company of warriors: riding, drinking wine, listening to the harp of the bard. And in the extended description of court life in Hrothgar's hall, we encounter more directly the high decorum of noble behavior, expressed in what were, for Germanic life, elaborate courtesies. There we also see the emphasis, as in Homeric epic, on open hospitality to guests and, above all, the joyous camaraderie the *gedryht* [troop] felt when feasting in their lord's hall. The traditional songs of the bard, chanted to the accompaniment of his harp, are so placed in these descriptions that they seem the natural climax of the happy tumult, an outpouring of the company's feelings of harmony by their most articulate spokesman.

We must expect some exaggeration and simplification in any picture of the past. In reality, Anglo-Saxon *œpelingas* did not spend all their time either in the mead-hall or in battle. They did have wives and families. Women in this aristocratic society, as in our poem, had all the dignity and standing they commanded in Tacitus's day: "they believe that there resides in women an element of holiness and prophecy, and so they do not scorn to ask their advice or lightly disregard

ANGLO-SAXON CHRISTIANITY AND REVENGE

In this excerpt from her well-known study The Audience of Beowulf, *Dorothy Whitelock argues that the Anglo-Saxon Christian Church was very tolerant of older customs concerning feuds and revenge.*

The audience [of *Beowulf*] is assumed to be interested in the blood-feud, to judge by the frequent references to stories which turn on this motive. If this implies a people not fully weaned from heathen ethics, the same could be said with equal justice of the Anglo-Saxons throughout their history. For the duty of protecting one's kindred, or one's lord, or one's man, and of exacting retribution from the slayer and his kindred if any of these were killed, was not superseded by Christianity. Action by the kindred, or, in special circumstances, by other persons empowered to act in their place, was the only means by which Anglo-Saxon law dealt with homicide until after the Norman Conquest. It is true that the Church threw the weight of its authority to support the practice of settling feuds by the payment of wergilds [substantial fines] instead of by the actual taking of vengeance, and that the law tried to put some pressure on the offender to make him pay composition for his deed. But even if the combined efforts of Church and State had been completely effective, there would remain the problem of the poor man of a poor kindred, who could not pay the wergild. Was such a person to be allowed to kill with impunity? In such cases, and also when, as frequently happened, passions were too enraged for peaceful settlement to be acceptable, the vengeance was allowed to take its course. . . . Killing for the sake of vengeance was not felt to be incompatible with Christian ethics at any period in Anglo-Saxon times.

their replies." (A good example is Queen Wealhtheow's dignified, poignant plea to Hrothgar about his sons' succession to the throne (1169–87). Wealhtheow and the other female characters have genuine status at court, as did noblewomen in real life. Sometimes they were "peace-weavers," given in diplomatic marriage to an enemy tribe, which could lead to tragic situations, as in the cases of Finn's queen, Hildeburh, and Hrothgar's daughter, Freawaru. Noblewomen in Anglo-Saxon society, as in the poem, possessed their own goods. There are important Anglo-Saxon queens in history from the seventh century on, some of whom played power politics, others who became abbesses of great foundations, and any number of lesser noblewomen who are named in land charters. On the whole, women probably had an even larger role in the day-to-day life of the core class than they do in *Beowulf*, where the poet uses them mainly to create an impression of splendid civility and heroic pathos. . . .

ANGLO-SAXON RULERS

Although no commoner receives extended attention in the poem, heroic obligations to one's lord were felt by *eorl* and *ceorl* alike in real life. It was a faithful swineherd, for instance, who first avenged the death of Cynewulf's ealdorman by killing King Sigebryht in A.D. 755. That event illustrates how easily this cohesive bond transcended class distinctions and also suggests the relatively small size of the early Anglo-Saxon kingdoms, whose population numbered only in tens of thousands. The kings exercised a high degree of direct, personal control, and . . . either they exercised it fully or other strong nobles would try to step into their place. Legitimacy, especially in the early days of the Anglo-Saxon settlement, was based mainly on strength, and even a strong body of kinsmen was not a sure guarantee of a peaceful succession, since an ambitious chief might lurk among them, waiting his chance. It has been pointed out that in Bede's *Ecclesiastical History* as well as in *Beowulf* the pivot of strife was usually a contest between uncle (father's brother) and nephew. The dynastic struggle described in *Beowulf* between the Swedish king Onela and his nephews Eanmund and Eadgils, and the future treachery of the Danish prince Hrothulf, Hrothgar's nephew, read like scenarios for the bloody struggle mentioned by Bede between King Hlothere of Kent and his nephew Eadric or the story of the gracious and saintly Oswin, murdered in A.D. 651 at the command of his treacherous cousin Oswy.

Such abominations were not the norm, but nonetheless the world of the Anglo-Saxons was turbulent enough that both *Beowulf* and Bede, and undoubtedly the common man, set great store on true virtue in kings. Peace was difficult enough to keep in any case, during the seventh and ninth centuries especially. A king of however small an area, if he were strong, just, and wise enough to keep war from breaking out, was a treasure beyond gold. Thus, when Beowulf dies, it is poetically appropriate that the Geats do not use the dragon's treasure to buy peace from their enemies, but bury it with Beowulf in honor of their priceless king. They act from one of the deepest pieties in the heroic life, and one that was not too distant from actuality. King Edwin of Northumbria ruled so well, Bede writes, that "the proverb still runs that a woman could carry her new-born babe across the island from sea to sea without any fear of harm. And such was the king's concern for the welfare of his people, that in a number of places where he had noticed clear springs adjacent to the highway, he ordered posts to be erected with brass bowls hanging from them, so that travelers could drink and refresh themselves. And so great was the people's affection for him, and so great the awe in which he was held, that no one presumed to use these bowls for any other purpose. The king's dignity was highly respected throughout his realm, and whether in battle or on a peaceful progress through city, town, and countryside in the company of his thanes, the royal standard was always borne before him." A similar standard is given Beowulf by Hrothgar in recognition of his victory and his preeminent suitability for kingship (1020–21). A more important parallel with Edwin is that Beowulf, once he is king, keeps the Geats safe from enemy attack for fifty years (Edwin ruled for seventeen). Beowulf is much beloved by his people, and when he dies, chaos again breaks loose, as it did for the Northumbrians after Edwin was slain. At the end of the poem, the mourners' insistence on Beowulf's fairness and kindness quite overburdens his heroic epitaph.

The Pessimism of Many Germanic Stories

A. Kent Hieatt

Though *Beowulf* is the earliest heroic epic surviving
in Old English, it is part of a wider Germanic literary
tradition. Some of the same heroes and incidents
appear in different stories. According to longtime
Columbia professor A. Kent Hieatt, however, what
unites this literary tradition more than anything else
is the shared emphasis on loyalty and the ethic of
revenge. For Hieatt, even the heroes in these stories
prove unable to break the pattern of vengeance,
resulting in a frequently tragic and always pessimistic view of life.

It is only in two strictly speaking nonliterary respects that
most Germanic narratives–Old English, Icelandic saga, the
Nibelungenlied[1]—share something important with *Beowulf.*
A reader needs to know about these points in order to understand the poem. The first of these is the frequent similarity
of narrative motifs—much the same heroes, much the same
incidents—often appearing in widely separated times and
places. The Germanic peoples seem to have inherited a common body of narrative, which is a key to understanding the
often incomplete and puzzling allusions and interpolated
stories forming a large part of *Beowulf.* The other feature
which *Beowulf* shares with other Germanic narratives is an
emphasis upon the ethical principle of loyalty to another—
to friend, family, chieftain, tribe, or the company of all faithful Christians. . . . The breaking of this bond through cowardice or treachery is considered singularly abominable;
and personally executed revenge—no matter how long
delayed, no matter how sanguinary [bloodthirsty]—against
the ones who harm one's associates is held to be mandatory

---

1. A Middle High German epic composed around A.D. 1200.

for every man, unless he is to be shamed publicly and even to hate himself. The typical tragedy of the Icelandic sagas is that of the good and far-seeing man who will not stir for small causes, even when his wife taunts him and his sons press weapons into his hands, but who, knowing he will sooner or later be murdered in turn, will kill coldly and kill again when this vengeful necessity of his manhood and fame is finally thrust upon him by the folly of others. In the same way, the pathos of the *Nibelungenlied* lies in the working out of a devious pattern of mutual vengeance through hecatombs of [a great deal of] frightful slaughter. The author himself sees that loyalty so understood is self-defeating, but he shows us no alternative. The Old English poems adapting Old Testament materials often center around much the same idea of vengeance: for example, the heroine of *Judith* cuts Holofernes' throat as a revenge for the Israelites, Satan revenges himself on God by attempting to destroy mankind, and God revenges himself on the Egyptians for the sake of his chosen people.

LOYALTY AND VENGEANCE

Liberal opinion is, of course, in full flight from this general principle, although each of us must recognize its force, inwardly in himself and outwardly in the feud, in the vendetta, and in much of the history of our own country and the world. We know that this principle is taken for granted in any society organized tribally and in terms of bloodlines and lacking legal remedy. Loyalty and bloody deeds of vengeance are preoccupations in much of the world's literature, not least in the later, feudal Middle Ages. . . . But Germanic story probably makes more of this doubtful ideal than does any other narrative tradition.

Beowulf, admittedly, shares in this doctrine of particular loyalties and of personal and social vengeance, and in the literary habit of extracting pathos from these patterns, but with a vital difference. In *Beowulf* alone these ideals appear in a partly sublimated and palatable form—institutionalized, so to speak, and harnessed into the service of a permanently acceptable view of man's lot, not of our primitive urges solely.

Beowulf's own loyalty, it is true, is literally tribal and familial. In the foreground of the story, the young hero, a nephew of the king of the Geats in Sweden, goes to the Danes, with whose kings he has connections, destroys the

> **A LARGELY ANGLO-SAXON WORLD**
>
> *In this excerpt from his recent book* Thinking About Beowulf, *James W. Earl muses that the issues and concerns of our world may not be so very different from Anglo-Saxon issues and concerns.*

We still live in a largely Anglo-Saxon world, and even over a millennium the child is father to the man. Different as we have become from the Anglo-Saxons and from each other, in our cultural origins we still sometimes see stark enlargements of our deepest traits, which otherwise go unobserved—though they have hardly disappeared for all that. The hall may have become the office, its rituals a system of contracted salaries, duties, and taxes, the wars corporate (or even academic); but the relations of such traditionally male-dominated institutions to women, the family, and religion remain as teasingly unresolved as ever and are still the subject of much of our literature. So too the broken oath, the failed promise, the conflict of loyalties, the silent hero, the alienation of the individual from society, and the problematic roles of women and kinship in social life.

These are the great Germanic themes—Germanic, more than biblical or classical. Our modern English-speaking world is indebted to those three traditions equally, and the Germanic leg of this cultural triad is firmly rooted in *Beowulf.*

Dane-devouring monster Grendel, destroys Grendel's mother (who has executed an unlooked-for vengeance herself), returns to the Geats, serves his king and the latter's successors, becomes king himself, and in his old age kills and is killed by a dragon who had been destroying the Geats. In the background of the story, the hero is even caught up in self-destructive tribal war, just as certain loyal warriors of the *Nibelungenlied* or a wife-ridden Icelandic hero is drawn into the execution of vengeance. Beowulf fights the Frisians because his rash king leads him among them; he fights the Swedes because his tribe has inherited a pattern of vengeance and countervengeance against them.

THE HERO'S ULTIMATE OVERTHROW

In reality, however, this pattern of personal and tribal loyalties is generalized. The *Beowulf* author's intention is to define the preeminent man as such, who is generous and helpful to those around him and gains his fame by such acts.

In the foreground he fights the enemies of us all, not simply of his friend, his family, or his tribe. He fights the fundamental forms of evil and harm, the descendants of the life-destroyer Cain—Grendel and his mother, envious of all human joy—and then the fire dragon, full of anger against man. He ostensibly avenges the harm done to the Danes in the one case and to his own Geats in the other, but the forms against which the vengeance flows out are mythical shorthand for what hurts all of us; they are not human enemies (as they are in most Germanic narratives) whose destruction might involve him in self-defeat or, as we say, in guilt. In other senses as well Beowulf is the one man in the poem who will *not* provoke the evils with which we hurt ourselves. He is the one who is not disloyal to his king, not treacherous towards his king's wife and son upon the king's demise, not ungenerous and murderous when he is a king himself, not cowardly—all things which others are guilty of in some dimension of the poem's curious allusiveness.

What is just as important, however, is that beyond all this he is not the bringer of a millennium [a new era], either, nor can anyone be, in the universe of the poem. The insistence upon the hero's ultimate overthrow is one of the work's most valuable heritages from the body of Germanic narrative. Beowulf resists evil for a time, but what hurts us, finally kills him as he is in the act of killing one of its forms. The two peoples whom he has principally benefited are both to be destroyed by their folly and others' vengeance. The ethical life of the poem, then, depends upon the propositions that evil can sometimes be truly identified, that those who fight it are good and those who conquer forms of it are wonderful, but that finally the evil that is part of this life is too much for the preeminent man, as it is for all the rest of us. The object of our vengeance is to destroy what hurts all of us, not to perpetuate more that is hurtful; but, justly maintaining that after all our efforts doom is there for all of us, the Beowulf is enabled to capitalize on the mighty pessimism of Germanic story.

Differences Between Modern and Anglo-Saxon Values

Fred C. Robinson

In this wide-ranging overview of Anglo-Saxon customs and values, noted *Beowulf* scholar Fred C. Robinson focuses on six areas in which these values differ widely from modern values, including differences concerning love and friendship, the concept of a "shame" culture, and the importance of the idea of fate. A longtime professor of English at Yale University, Robinson is the author of *Beowulf and the Appositive Style* (1985).

Instead of reviewing scholarly investigations of the cultural background of *Beowulf,* the general reader may find it useful to examine a few of the instances where a theme or subject in *Beowulf* had markedly different cultural significance for the poet and his audience than it has for the modern student of the poem. Consideration of six such topics will help readers free themselves from their own cultural preconceptions and project themselves into the imaginative world of *Beowulf:* love and friendship, shame culture and guilt culture, vengeance, descriptions of artifacts and nature, gift giving, and fate.

LOVE AND FRIENDSHIP

Our first instance of a cultural conflict between Anglo-Saxon and modern worlds is not precisely a subject dealt with in *Beowulf* but one that is conspicuously missing from it. Although women as well as men figure importantly in the narrative and although a husband's love (or the cooling of his love) is mentioned once (2065–66), romantic passion between the sexes is absent from *Beowulf,* as it is absent from most Old English poetry, while feelings of friendship and loyalty between men are surprisingly intense. C.S. Lewis in *The Allegory of Love* has characterized the Germanic attitude toward love and friendship in the Middle Ages:

> "Love," in our sense of the word, is as absent from the litera-ture of the Dark Ages as from that of classical antiqui-ty. . . . The deepest of worldly emotions in this period is the love of man for man, the mutual love of warriors who die together fighting against odds, and the affection between vas-sal and lord. We shall never understand this last, if we think of it in the light of our own moderated and impersonal loyal-ties. . . . The feeling is more passionate and less ideal than our patriotism. . . . Of romance, of reverence for women, of the idealizing imagination exercised about sex, there is hardly a hint. The centre of gravity is elsewhere—in the hopes and fears of religion, or in the clean and happy fidelities of the feudal hall. . . .

Lewis may overdramatize the distinction between medieval and modern attitudes, but the distinction is there and must be remembered when we read of Beowulf's farewell from Hrothgar (1870–80) or of his expression of affection for Hygelac (2149–51). We should also remember Lewis' words when we read the description of Beowulf at the end of the poem. Readers have often assumed that since the hero has no heir and since no wife is mentioned we are to understand that he remained solitary and celibate throughout his life. It is quite possible, however, that the poet simply felt that Beowulf's marital status was of insufficient interest to war-rant mention in the poem.

SHAME CULTURE

In *The Greeks and the Irrational* (17–18) E.R. Dodds adopts the anthropologists' terms shame culture and guilt culture to explain an important difference between the outlook of the heroic age and a later day. The highest good in a society like that of Homer or Beowulf is public esteem and the greatest evil is public disgrace. . . . Beowulf says as much in lines 1386–89. The public dispute with Unferth, the obsession with fame, the hero's concern for his memorial after his death, all should be viewed in the light of the fact that Beowulf lived in a shame culture. The Christian society of the poet and his audience, on the other hand, is a guilt culture, where the highest good is the enjoyment of a quiet conscience. In the poem *Beowulf,* then, we have a shame culture as viewed through the eyes of a guilt culture, and at one point the contrast between the two comes to the surface. When Beowulf asks himself whether the dragon's attacks can be the result of some unrecognized wrongdoing on his part, the poet observes, "His breast within was troubled with dark thoughts, *which was not usual with him*" (2331–32). The heroic world is a world of action and of public recognition for deeds performed, not of brooding and soul searching.

One form of public esteem sought by Germanic man is revealed in the ritual of revenge. Each man sought to demonstrate that injury done to him or to any of his people would have to be remedied or vengeance would be taken. Francis Bacon defined revenge as "a kind of wild justice," but in the ancient Germanic world it was an exceedingly precise and elaborate kind of justice. Traditional laws prescribed that if a person is killed or injured by another, then the injuring party must offer to the victim's lord an amount of compensation precisely calibrated according to the predetermined worth of the victim. Otherwise life will be taken in talion for life. This system of organized retribution protected the weak against injury and the strong against loss of esteem. When the system breaks down, the result is extreme anguish—as when the Danes have to suffer Grendel's depredations without restitution (154–58) or when Hrethel must see his son die unavenged (2442–43). In these instances the survivors must bitterly accept their bereavement with no outlet for grief.

THE GIVING OF GIFTS

Another feature of Beowulfian society that is related to the importance of public esteem is the giving of gifts. Scene after scene in the royal halls shows king and retainer giving and receiving gold, weapons, horses, accoutrements, grants of land, and other items of great value. Early in the poem (20–25) the poet remarks how important it is for young kings to be generous with gifts, and much of Hrothgar's long speech to Beowulf in lines 1700–84 is devoted to the importance of generosity. In large part this emphasis is a function of a culture oriented toward fame and shame. Receiving a splendid gift is a visible sign of a man's worth, and since visible recognition is the central good in this society, the deserving men must receive rewards. It is the act of giving and receiving that is important more than the actual possession of the gift. Often in *Beowulf* a gift received is promptly presented to another person, as when Queen Wealhtheow gives Beowulf a splendid torque and he, on his return to Geatland, promptly gives it to the Geatish royal family. Gift taking also had social and ceremonial significance, being an overt symbol of the social contract implicit in the heroic world. When a man receives a gift from his lord or queen, for example, he solemnizes his allegiance to the dispenser of the gift. For a man to accept a gift and then fail his benefactor in time of need would not merely be ingratitude; it would be a violation of the social code. Beyond these symbolic aspects of gift giving, moreover, the *Beowulf* poet seems to imply an even more elemental good in openhandedness, as if it were a measure of one's well-being. There is warmth and joy in the scenes of gift giving and a reassuring sense that social harmony is attainable. Negative examples like the niggardly Heremod, on the other hand, suggest that stinginess is a sign of almost pathological unhappiness. The *Beowulf* poet would have found it fitting that the modern English word "misery" is derived from "miser."

Any reader of *Beowulf* will be struck by the poet's frequent and enthusiastic descriptions of artifacts: sword hilts, saddles, shields, jewelry, and helmets are all carefully depicted, and the building of Heorot is described as if it were the crowning achievement of Hrothgar's kingship. While it is true that archaeological discoveries like Sutton Hoo have revealed remarkable craftsmanship among Anglo-Saxon smiths, jewelers, and metalworkers, one might think nonetheless that so much attention to artifacts in *Beowulf* bespeaks an almost childish preoccupation with material objects. But this impression would result from a conflict in medieval and modern cultural values. Rousseau and the English Romantic writers have taught us to mistrust the artificial products of a calculating mind and to put our trust in nature—an external nature that is benign and instructive and a human nature that is inherently good. But to medieval people and the poet of *Beowulf* nature is chaotic and menacing. The few descriptions we get of nature are almost entirely of storms, fire, and the frightening mere. Grendel emerges from fens that are swarming with natural and reptilian life. Each artifact that the *Beowulf* poet describes is reassurance that mankind can control the natural world, can constrain its brute substance into pattern and order. . . .

The conduct of human beings is formalized into banqueting rituals, social forms, traditions, and patterns of allegiance, thus bringing human nature as well as external nature into reassuring patterns. It is in the light of this desire for rational order as a defense against the anarchy of nature that we should read the description of artifacts in *Beowulf.* Each celebration of a damascened sword or a well-constructed helmet recapitulates in miniature that moment early in the poem when Hrothgar builds Heorot—when a good king brings order to a people and a place by walling out the beasts and fens and darkness and constructing a place of control and assembly whose "light shone over many lands."

THE CONCEPT OF FATE

The common Old English word for "fate" is *wyrd,* a word that is still used by Shakespeare when he refers to the "weird sisters" (i.e., the sisters of fate) in *Macbeth. Wyrd* is mentioned repeatedly in *Beowulf* as the force determining lives, and some scholars have thought that behind these usages lurks the old pagan idea of the Germanic goddess of fate. The plural of *wyrd* is used by other writers to translate Latin *Parcae,* the name of the Roman mythological goddesses of fate, so clearly *wyrd* did have this association, but most scholars think that in *Beowulf* the term refers to fate in a more abstract sense. In his translation of Boethius's *Consolation of Philosophy* King Alfred reasons from a Christian viewpoint that *wyrd* is the accomplishment of God's providence. That is, *wyrd* is subject to God, it is what God determines shall be. In *Beowulf, wyrd* and God are mentioned as parallel and simultaneous forces at times, which would seem to support the Boethian reading of the concept in the poem. But quite possibly the term is to be understood according to context. To the characters in the poem, their lives seem to be governed by a stern and implacable fate. Both the poet and his audience knew that that fate, *wyrd,* was simply the accomplishment of God's will, but they also knew that to Beowulf and his contemporaries, who were deprived of Christian revelation, *wyrd* represented something more obscure and disquieting.

These aspects of the world of *Beowulf* that have meanings different from those our modern culture would lead us to expect are only representative of a larger number of such subjects requiring modern readers to question their cultural assumptions as they read the poem. Understanding literature from another time and land is an exercise in projecting ourselves imaginatively into other people's minds and lives and language. It is this exercise that constitutes one of the greatest rewards of literary study, as one thinks one's way into a different time and a different world from one's own. The world of *Beowulf* is worth the effort.

CHAPTER 2

The Heroic Character of Beowulf

The Conflicting Demands of Heroic Strength and Kingly Wisdom

John Leyerle

The Anglo-Saxon heroic code glories in individual achievement, while the institution of kingship requires a leader who will put the good of his people first. In the following essay, *Beowulf* scholar John Leyerle spells out the implications of these contradictory roles and expectations. As a hero who is also a king, Beowulf falls short, unable to fulfill two incompatible roles. According to Leyerle, at the end of the poem Beowulf chooses heroic glory, and consequently leaves his people leaderless and at risk.

The interlace narrative of *Beowulf* is hard to follow unless one is told what the pattern is in abstract language, exactly the kind of statement the poet rightly avoids. The purpose of this article is to examine the episodes of the poem, to show how they are connected to produce structural unity, and to elucidate the major theme. This theme is the fatal contradiction at the core of heroic society. The hero follows a code that exalts indomitable will and valour in the individual, but society requires a king who acts for the common good, not for his own glory. The greater the hero, the more likely his tendency to imprudent action as king. The three battles with the monsters, the central episodes in the poem, reveal a pattern in which Beowulf's pre-eminence as a hero leads to the destruction of the Geats when he becomes king. This pattern is apparent in the motivation and actions of the monsters whose force increases as their reasons for fighting become better justified.

Grendel is an unblessed creature descended from Cain and condemned by the Creator. He bears God's wrath . . . and he is called "God's adversary" (786). Grendel's situ-

This article is an extract of about half of John Leyerle's article, "Beowulf the Hero and the King," which was first published in *Medium Aevum*, 34 (1965), pp. 89-102. The translations from the Old English original text in Klaeber's edition were prepared by John Leyerle for this volume. Reprinted by permission of *Medium Aevum*.

ation explains his anger at the joy in Heorot. His attack is provoked by the rejoicing of the Danes at the completion of their hall and by their praise of God's creation; these would offend no ordinary creature. He kills thirty men on his first attack. His man-like form makes him particularly horrible, for he is not so much a beast as a cannibal in devouring his victims. Grendel is opposed to God, evil incarnate, and his destruction by Beowulf is a triumph of heroic goodness over devilish evil. Grendel is less powerful than Beowulf in fighting. Once Beowulf seizes him, he realizes that he is in the grip of a much stronger warrior. With a wail of defeat, he flees from the contest fatally wounded. The battle is never in doubt, for Beowulf's strength is overwhelming.

In attacking Heorot, Grendel's mother is concerned only to avenge her son and she kills only one man. The motivation of Grendel's mother and the single slaying that results would seem justified to an Anglo-Saxon audience. Blood feuds continued throughout the Anglo-Saxon period . . . and vengeance was a powerful obligation. The motive of Grendel's mother is acceptable to the codes of men. The battle in the mere is almost even and Beowulf kills his enemy only after he nearly loses his own life.

In the third battle the pattern is completed. The dragon is aroused to action by the theft of a precious cup from his hoard, and Beowulf is killed in the ensuing fight. The theft probably brings into effect the curse on the gold mentioned in ll. 3051–57, but passages in the poem about the origins of the hoard present notorious difficulties of interpretation. No connected history of the hoard can be reconstructed with any certainty. Whatever the forces of the curse, the dragon, like Grendel's mother, is little concerned with the affairs of men until given offence. He guards the treasure quietly for three hundred years until a slave steals a cup. Then he retaliates. His retribution is in kind, for he destroys property as the result of the theft of property.

The nature of the dragon is important to any critical judgement of the poem and has been given considerable attention since Tolkien, the poem's most influential critic, focused attention on the monsters. Tolkien regarded the dragon as a creature 'more evil than any human enemy of house or realm'. He argued that the three monsters are 'of a similar order and kindred significance'. An objection was raised to this interpretation by T.M. Gang, who pointed out that the dragon is nowhere referred to as being hateful to God. He is

. . . cruel, malicious, and generally destructive to men and their work, but that is not the same as being God's enemy like Grendel. The dragon dies fighting in defence of a narrow place, the entrance to his underground barrow—a classic stance of the Germanic hero. The sea receives the dragon's body in contrast to Grendel's consignment to hell. . . . The Geats push the body of the dragon into the sea as they would launch a longship. A vindication of the dragon must not go too far, but clearly he is not an evil creature like Grendel, but rather a destructive force of nature functioning like an agent of fate.

The motivations and actions of the monsters make a clear pattern. Grendel, the evil offspring of Cain, attacks Heorot because songs in praise of creation anger him. He devours the flesh, blood and bones of many Danes wantonly. Beowulf waits for him in Heorot and wounds him fatally when he attacks. Grendel's mother, also evil, leaves her lair impelled by the duty of blood vengeance, an obligation that was almost necessity in heroic society, and kills one man. She, in turn, is attacked and killed in her underwater hall. Finally the dragon takes retribution for a theft by burning buildings, probably under the compulsion of an ancient curse. He is attacked and destroyed at the door of his hall, killing Beowulf in the battle. As the motivation of the monsters becomes better justified, their force increases. The high points of the poem are these three battles in which the behaviour of the monsters makes an apparent pattern that corresponds to a reciprocal pattern in the behaviour of Beowulf. His force against the monsters decreases. This much is clear. The fact that his actions become less justified is not. . . .

HROTHGAR'S WARNING

After Beowulf's victory over Grendel, the "king's thegn began skilfully to tell about Beowulf's mission" (867-73) by recounting the deeds of Sigemund in juxtaposition with those of Heremod. Later Hrothgar praises Beowulf in words dear to the heart of a Germanic hero: "You have yourself performed such feats that your fame will live for all time" (953-55).

That night Grendel's mother avenges her son and Hrothgar summons Beowulf next day to ask his aid against the new threat, if he dares. Beowulf agrees at once, answering without reflection. . . After the death of Grendel's mother, Hrothgar's debt to Beowulf is doubled. Already he has praised him mightily and declared that his fame would live forever. What greater eulogy could the king give?

He ponders the golden sword hilt for the longest dramatic pause in the poem before saying a few words of praise. Then, as Hrothgar's thegn had done, he turns to heroic legend. He ignores Sigemund's story, but gives Heremod's specific relevance to Beowulf. . . .

Beowulf's behaviour at the Danish court is such that it prompts the thegn to allude to Heremod, and Hrothgar to make the relevance to Beowulf specific in a pointed warning after his second victory. In blunt language his discourse contains a warning on the ease with which pride . . . can grow and flourish in a man given great authority, as Beowulf would one day have. Hrothgar sees in Beowulf's behaviour in Denmark a tendency to unreflective confidence in his own strength, to impetuosity in acting, and to excessive concern for praise, *lof*, causing the king to caution Beowulf in his moment of triumph in Heorot.

Beowulf returns home and Hygelac expresses his earlier opposition to Beowulf's expedition against Grendel: "I long entreated you in no way to attack Grendel, that bloodthirsty demon, but let the South-Danes on their own settle their score with him" (1994-97).

These words make an interesting contrast with the information given early in the poem. . . . Beowulf summarizes the advice given to him in Geatland in his speech to Hrothgar in Heorot soon after his arrival (415–18), but passes in silence the fact that he had disregarded the opposition to the expedition by king Hygelac, his uncle. The omission is not indicated until the second half of the poem after Hrothgar had given an explicit comment on his impression of Beowulf's tendency to rash, unreflective action and pride in his own strength. The poet glances at one reason why Beowulf is particularly sensitive about his honour in ll. 2183–88. Despised and unhonoured in his early youth, he prizes his reputation with the passion of a man cherishing that which has been denied him. . . .

BEOWULF'S RASH ATTITUDE

Time passes and Hygelac is killed in a rash attack on Frisia, instigated "because of pride". His beach force is annihilated, except for Beowulf, who escapes to tell the story. . . .After a succession of wars, which arouse the enmity of the neighbouring people, the kingship falls to Beowulf. . . .

The situations are similar, but Beowulf does not emulate the long-enduring restraint of Hrothgar and is not warned by Hygelac's example. He undertakes precipitant action himself, the last of the fool-hardy deeds attributed to him by Wiglaf: "Our lord, the guardian of the people, thought to finish this bold deed single-handedly, because he, most of all men, had carried out the greatest and most rash of deeds" (2642–46). The dragon, little more than an agent of fate, presents the inevitable challenge to Beowulf's heroic susceptibilities.

He prepares himself for battle and orders a special iron shield, but he disdains the use of an adequate force against the dragon. . . .Outside the barrow, Beowulf does not allow the twelve men with him to help and undertakes single combat. The first rush is inconclusive. The cowardly retainers flee to the woods and only the valiant Wiglaf joins the battle to aid his lord.

As Wiglaf enters the fight, his words to Beowulf are surprising and significant. . . . He urges the king to save his life. An individual hero might properly ignore risk to himself, as the poet indicates during Beowulf's fight with Grendel's mother, but not a king, least of all one in Beowulf's situation. . . .

With Beowulf's death, Wiglaf comes to the Geatish throne wearing his father's sword, the weapon that had killed Eanmund. A sword that instigates a man to take revenge by opening old wounds and grievances is a familiar motif in northern literature. It is explicit in the Finnsburg and Heathobard episodes and implicit in the hints about the hostilities that are to follow Beowulf's death and destroy the Geats. . . .

THE WEAKNESS OF HEROIC SOCIETY

The poem presents a criticism of the essential weakness of the society it portrays. . . . Heroic society inevitably encouraged a king to act the part of a hero, yet the heroic king, however glorious, was apt to be a mortal threat to his nation. An individual's desire for glory . . . becomes an increasingly dangerous motivation as a man's responsibility for leadership grows. Even without such desire, a leader's excessive reliance on his personal strength easily brings calamity. . . .

Hrothgar's speech to Beowulf, lying at the centre of the

poem, is, in part, a caution against headlong action and excessive pride in a king. Hrothgar himself, the embodiment here of discretion and *mensura*, "proportion", is the nearest to an ideal king in the poem—not Beowulf. . . .

Beowulf does not heed the advice of Hrothgar nor the example of Hygelac's Frisian disaster. He fights the dragon in single combat, supposing that the death of the dragon and the acquisition of the gold hoard are the best benefits he can confer on his people. Wiglaf's comment on the outcome reveals that Beowulf disregards the advice of his counsellors who resolutely, if ineffectually, had opposed the encounter with the dragon. The technique of interlace narrative allows the poet to withhold this glance at the council of the Geats before the dragon fight until after Beowulf's death. The rash action of Beowulf brings affliction to many, as Wiglaf, quite specifically, says:

> Wiglaf, the son of Wihstan, spoke aloud, 'Often times many a noble must endure misery because of the wish of one man, as has happened to us. We could in no way give our dear lord, the guardian of the kingdom, any counsel that he not attack that gold keeper, but let him lie where he had long lived, stay in his barrow until the world's end.' (3076–83)

As all readers of the older literature of the north know, the individual code of unyielding will . . . has a compelling beauty that cannot be found in the bedroom world of Chaucer's *Troilus* or of *Gawain and the Green Knight*. Beowulf is a figure of grandeur, admirable in much. The trouble was that heroic society was inherently unstable, for men who had been accustomed to conduct suitable to an individual hero could not adjust to the rather different conduct suitable to a king. The end of the heroic age, like the end of the Geats, was not accidental. . . .

AN HEROIC, NOT CHRISTIAN SOCIETY

The Anglo-Saxons valued their continental ancestry and respected the heroic traditions of the north, although they knew that the Danes and Swedes were pagans. The society presented in *Beowulf* is regarded as existing under pre-Mosaic, natural law, hence the nature of the funerals, the religious lapse of the Danes, and the total absence of references to the New Testament or to anything in the Old Testament after the coming of Moses. The *Beowulf* poet has a Christian context which gives him perspective and distance in his clear understanding of heroic society. Yet he carefully avoids forcing that society into his Christian context. Consequently, caution is necessary in applying specifically Christian notions to *Beowulf* as if a Christian society were being described. Beowulf is no more a Christian prince than he is an example of *superbia* "pride". He is a worthy pagan and at his death his soul departs "to seek judgement from the truthful" (2820), a judgement based on "the old law" (2330), which, as M.W. Bloomfield has pointed out, refers to pre-Mosaic, natural law. Beowulf has many virtues and his calamity is the more moving because it arises from a fault inherent in the heroic age, a fault that is, quite literally, glorious. A man excellent in most things, he "strove for glory" (2179) and was too eager for praise: "the most mild and kind of men, the gentlest to his people, and the most eager for praise" (3181–82).

A king's unrestrained desire for individual glory was a particular danger in heroic society, although it remained a risk throughout the mediæval period. . . .

The funeral of Beowulf marks the start of terrible affliction for the Geats; without allies, beset by enemies, led by the inexperienced Wiglaf, who is the object of the personal vengeance of the Swedish king, they face exile or death. Records from the tenth century onward mention the Geats, showing that the implied annihilation of them in *Beowulf* is a poetic exaggeration, although it must have appeared close enough to actuality in the eighth century to satisfy the historical sense of an Anglo-Saxon audience.

All turns on the figure of Beowulf, a man of magnificence, whose understandable, almost inevitable pride commits him to individual, heroic action and leads to a national calamity by leaving his race without mature leadership at a time of extreme crisis, facing human enemies much more destructive than the dragon. His last act is to order his barrow: ". . . on the ocean cape; it will tower high on Whale's Headland as a memorial for my people" (2803–805).

This barrow becomes the cenotaph for his nation and functions less as a reminder to his people than for them. In *Beowulf* an heroic race suffers dire affliction largely through the heroic fault of its king; its memorials are a lonely barrow at the edge of the sea—and a poem.

The Corruption of Beowulf

Margaret E. Goldsmith

In this excerpt from her book *The Mode and Meaning of Beowulf,* British scholar Margaret E. Goldsmith argues that Beowulf's demise is due to his zeal for fame and treasure, a zeal stemming ultimately from excessive self-confidence and spiritual pride. Goldsmith contends that Beowulf's heroism, selfless and properly motivated in the first half of the story, evolves into a selfish quest for personal glory. His fall, in this view, should be understood as a spiritual allegory in which Beowulf reenacts the fall of mankind, falling prey to the temptation represented by the dragon's hoard.

The last lines of [*Beowulf*] praise the dead king in the words of his followers: as kind and gentle to all men, and as *lofgeornost* [most eager for praise]. That final controversial word leaves the hearer with a tacit question: did Beowulf do right to challenge the dragon alone? . . .

It has sometimes been argued that the word *lofgeornost* carries implications of excess, but one would not expect the king's followers to review his faults in their lament for him. This consideration, and the parallelism of the other superlative expressions, make the translation 'too eager for fame' inappropriate. Nevertheless, the word is double-edged, and may well be meant as dramatic irony, in view of Wiglaf's earlier censure of Beowulf's decision to go after the dragon and the forecast of a wretched future for the Geats as a consequence of his fatal combat. Beowulf's zeal for fame quite evidently proved calamitous to his people, and it may reasonably be thought an example of *desmesure* [excess], the opposite of the ideal of *mensura* [restraint] which [L.L] Schücking rightly recognized to be present in the poem.

Strangely, Schücking did not consider the possibility that Beowulf in the end fell short of the ideal. Yet the hero was at the best tragically wrong to suppose that his single combat with the dragon would benefit his people. If a worse construction is placed on his decision to fight alone for the treasure, it may be said that his heroic desire for glory was selfish and imprudent. The poet does not say this, nor does he praise him unequivocally for this act of heroism. In this way he brings the code of personal heroism into question.

A SELFISH QUEST

In the first part of the poem no questioning of ethical ideals is apparent. . . . But his early fame was won in willing service of his fellow-men, accompanied by trust in God, so that his heroic deeds did not contravene God's law. If he endangered his own life, he harmed no other person by so doing. After fifty years, he is in the very different situation of a man with power and responsibility. In secular terms, the heroic gesture may prove detrimental to his subjects. From a religious point of view, the search for fame which is the young prince was a part of loyal service to God and king, has become in the old ruler a much more selfish quest in which God is not acknowledged as the author of his strength and upholder of his power. Following this train of thought, one can see that the heroic gesture and its calamitous effect are what one would expect to stem from the spiritual deterioration described by Hrothgar. The unrecking challenge *per se* is a symptom of arrogant self-confidence, and if there is added to it a desire for gain, the hero's bold action is spiritually perilous.

. . . The symbolic persons in the old legends had to change their allegiances or cease to act as sources of inspiration. Some critics who have realized this fact have themselves read into the poem a change from the traditional hero's motives of eagerness for personal glory and gold to an eagerness to serve the people even at the risk of death. However, the text places an obstacle in the way of this interpretation, in that Beowulf's expressed motives as he goes to meet the dragon do not mention the people at all, though he says plainly enough that he means to win the gold or die and utters a great *beotword* [boast].

His concern for the people has to be inferred from what is said after the fatal combat. His own last words about the treasure are a thanksgiving "that I might have gained such gifts as these for the sake of my people before I died. . . ."

Wiglaf later attributes to him the intention of fighting alone for his men's sake. . . .

However, Wiglaf's words to the followers are mitigating the sting of their lord's earlier words to them—"it is not your business"—as the purpose of his harangue requires, and the impression it leaves of Beowulf's care for the men's welfare is much weakened by the same man's later speech regretting the misery which Beowulf's action will cause the people. . . .

Wiglaf's speeches are conditioned by the immediate rhetorical aim; the author himself does not make any objective pronouncement about the rightness of Beowulf's action or the true nature of his motives. But he goes out of his way to tell us that Beowulf saw the dragon's attack as a sign of God's anger upon himself. It is difficult not to conclude that Beowulf's boasting, his sense of God's anger, and his eagerness to set eyes on the treasure are signs of a more worldly outlook in the old king than in the young champion whom Hrothgar praised so highly. I would add to these indications the fact that he does not mention God before or during his last fight.

BEOWULF'S EXCESSIVE PRIDE

To ask whether Beowulf did right to challenge the dragon alone is to assume that the poem treats of moral choice; some critics, however, maintain that Beowulf's course is charted, and any other response to the dragon's invasion out of the question. . . .

[Stanley B.] Greenfield contends that the old Geatish king faced no dilemma; the code by which he lived could admit no other kind of action. This would be true if Beowulf exemplified only the ancient loyalties of the pagan warrior tribe. But because he has been re-created as the central figure in a history in which God himself intervenes, he must, like every human being, be held responsible to God for what he does. He does not act in ignorance of his duty to God, for Hrothgar has enlarged his natural understanding of the issues which he faces. The ethical pattern upon which the king's life is shaped is duplex, but its main elements can be kept in rough accord up to this point, at which the acceptance of excessive pride as a noble fault in the traditional hero is seen to be incompatible with the Christian belief that

THE WEAKNESS OF AGING MEN

In this excerpt from his book The Hero and the King: An Epic Theme, *W.T.H. Jackson suggests that it is really Beowulf's interior opponent, his avarice, that causes his demise, not the dragon.*

In the long run, Heorot cannot be saved. Internecine [mutually destructive] struggles will destroy it and it is not by any means certain that Beowulf's kingdom was not destroyed in a similar way. Beowulf has no trouble with the intruder from outside. It is the opponent from within who destroys him, and this opponent is the personification of wealth hoarded and not used for encouraging bravery and good conduct, as Hrothgar, to his credit, had used his. Avarice is the weakness of aging men, and the author may wish us to understand that it is not merely against outside forces that a king must contend. Even Beowulf, the ideal hero and king, is not fully proof against the vice of avarice, and his dying wish to see the treasure distributed may reflect his repentance.

excessive pride, which separates man from God, is the greatest sin. . . .

It could be contended that the heroic fault is necessary to the plot. Only Beowulf's disastrous self-sufficiency can account for his death and the affliction of the people in a world governed by an all-seeing and beneficent Lord who has twice preserved him from death in similar contests. Even so, *desmesure* could have been an element in a story of the killing of the dragon without the motive of treasure-winning. I cannot see that Beowulf's boast that he would obtain the treasure, or his dying wish to set eyes upon it, were necessary ingredients of the plot. It would have been becoming in the old king to seek to rid the land of the dragon, as he had rid Denmark of Grendel, and he might have been forgiven an excess of valour in attempting the task alone. The proud gesture at the end of his life is not . . . the expected culmination of an arrogant career, and the story could have been as fittingly concluded with a death of self-sacrifice. Some readers have found a selfless motive in Beowulf's decision to fight the dragon; obviously, therefore, the poet has not said very plainly that Beowulf went to his death because he was lured by thoughts of fame and the treasure. Even those who ascribe arrogance to him are loath to think of him as infected by cupidity. Nevertheless, it must be conceded that he shows great eagerness to see the treasure in his last hour, and the audience has been warned of the corruption of wealth as well as the spiritual dangers of power. His involvement with the treasure therefore asks for close scrutiny. . . .

AN ALLEGORY OF BEOWULF'S TEMPTATION

I return now to the matter of the hero's state of mind and spirit in his last hours, and to the allegorical significance of the dragon fight. I interpret this combat as an allegory of the temptation forecast in Hrothgar's warning speech. Like the earlier monster-fights this contest figures the hero's interior battle with the Devil. This time, the Enemy uses the gold to entice him away from "eternal gains," and the hero, unguarded for the reasons Hrothgar describes, is almost conquered. . . .

I would interpret the allegory like this: the rifling of the hoard, by exhibiting the dragon's costly cup to Beowulf and his men, lets loose the fiery breath of Leviathan through the kingdom. Beowulf suffers unwonted disturbance of mind and a sense of estrangement from God. He is enticed by thought of the treasure and the fame that will accrue to him if he wins it. His challenge to the dragon allegorically presents his attempts to repulse this thought, but he is already spiritually weakened by the feeling of self-sufficiency which long years of success have bred. Hence he goes into the fight foolishly trusting in his own strength, looking nether to man nor to God for help. He makes provision for the fight with a great iron shield, when what he needs is the shield of faith. On the historical level, this is simply making physical rather than spiritual preparation; allegorically, Beowulf's defence is his own justice. The iron shield protects him all too short a time; what saves him from utter defeat is the intervention of Wiglaf. . . .

THE TRAGEDY OF FALLEN MAN

It is thus reasonable to regard Beowulf as a just man who has fought the good fight during his lifetime, but who is in the end brought to death by the flaws in his human nature, the legacy of Adam's sin, in trying to fight the Dragon alone. He acts as a moral example in his early life, but in his last days he presents to the Christian audience the tragedy of fallen man, harassed by the Enemy and wanting [lacking] in the supernatural strength of the *miles Christi* [Christian soldier]. . . .

No part of Beowulf brings out so clearly the difference between Christian and non-Christian values as the hero's dying speeches. Though he is a righteous man, Beowulf's mind is occupied with *terenna* [earthly things]. . . .

The description of Beowulf's passing is designed both to celebrate the valour and nobility of a great hero of the past and to look with compassion upon the limited horizons and misdirected aims of the unregenerate sons of Adam. As Dante with Ulysses, so our poet with Beowulf admired the unbending spirit of the old king and yet acknowledged that without divine aid the hero could not win eternal life.

Beowulf's Heroic Death

J.D.A. Ogilvy and Donald C. Baker

Beowulf's behavior at the end of the poem and his subsequent death have been blamed variously on his spiritual pride, his excessive zeal for fame, and on his greed for the dragon's gold. Scholars J.D.A. Ogilvy and Donald C. Baker contend, however, that Beowulf's behavior is admirable to the end, and that his heroic death is not marred by character flaws. They argue that Beowulf embodies a valiant stoicism, dying unselfishly in service to his people. Ogilvy and Baker are well-known scholars of medieval literature and coauthors of *Reading Beowulf: An Introduction.*

[Near the end of *Beowulf,*] the author describes Beowulf and the dragon lying dead side by side and observes rather sententiously that it was a bad business fighting with a dragon or disturbing his hoard. Beowulf, he adds, had paid for the treasure with his life. Some commentators seem to consider this passage, combined with Wiglaf's remarks about Beowulf's insistence on fighting the dragon alone, as a criticism of Beowulf's conduct. Beowulf's tactics may be open to criticism, but it is hard to see how he could have saved his people without fighting the dragon, and this was not an age in which a commander "led his regiment from behind." It is true that the poet shifts the emphasis of his tale from Beowulf's defense of his realm to his winning of the dragon's hoard, but he can hardly have forgotten Beowulf's original purpose. Possibly he felt that Beowulf realized that his people would need treasure after he was gone. . . .

THE DRAGON'S CURSE

With his customary impartiality the author then goes on to blame the dragon: "Then it was plain that it did not profit him who unrighteously hid treasure within a wall. The

Reprinted by permission of the University of Oklahoma Press from *Reading "Beowulf": An Introduction to the Poem, Its Background, and Its Style,* by J.D.A. Ogilvy and Donald C. Baker. Copyright © 1983 by the University of Oklahoma, Norman, Publishing Division of the University.

guardian had slain one of a few; then the feud was swiftly avenged." Next the author embroiders an idea also found in an Arab saying: "No man knoweth where his grave is dug" (lines 3062b–65). Beowulf did not know when he challenged the dragon how his end would come. Considering that he depicts Beowulf as fey [full of foreboding] throughout the first part of this episode, the author seems to be contradicting himself as in one or two other passages in which he indulges in incremental repetition. Having begun with a straightforward dragon fight in the Sigemund manner, he bethinks him that there may have been a spell or curse involved. He does, however, put in an escape clause "Thus the mighty lords who put that [the treasure] there solemnly declared that that man who disturbed that place should be guilty of sin, harried by a pagan curse, fast in the bonds of hell, tormented by evil *unless the one desirous of gold was assured of the Lord's favor"* (italics ours, lines 3069–75).

Twice in this passage (lines 3054–57, 3074–75) the author implies that the Lord can cancel the curse, just as he states . . . that the Lord granted Beowulf victory over Grendel. Since there is nothing anywhere else in the poem to imply that Beowulf is destined for the bonds of hell, we must assume that the curse has been at least partly negated. That it was completely so and that Beowulf's fate is simply a consequence of the dragon's *ellen* [bravery] is a possible, if somewhat strained, interpretation. Another—also not entirely satisfactory—is that the curse, though negated in the hereafter, has retained some residual force in the here. The most plausible is that, like Homer, the author occasionally nods and that this is one of those occasions. A further inconsistency is that in the first account of the burying of the treasure there are no "might lords" but only one wretched survivor and that his speech contains no spell or curse.

A DECLINE IN MORALE

When the cowardly retainers return, they are bitterly rebuked by Wiglaf, who then sends a messenger to inform the people of Beowulf's death. It is extremely unlikely that Wiglaf, who seems to have been a young man of some promise, would actually have sent such a bird of ill omen at a time when the Geats needed to gather all their strength and resolution to meet attacks that were sure to come. Plainly the author is using the messenger as a means to foreshadow the fate that he knew would soon overtake the Geats.

The messenger announces Beowulf's death and goes on to prophesy war with the Franks and the Swedes. In a long, rather difficult passage he relates the death of Ongentheow at the hands of the Geats. Not content with this, he says that all the treasure of the dragon's hoard will be laid on the pyre because the days of the Geats' power are over and nothing awaits them but poverty, captivity, exile, and death. Any commander who knew his business would, of course, have silenced this "wise man," as the poet calls him, with a noose around the neck.

Perhaps the poet wishes to show a decline in Geatish morale in the last section of the poem. Except for Wiglaf, Beowulf's retainers in the dragon fight are a sorry contrast to the thanes who stoically prepared to die with him in Heorot. An overconscientious commentator might speculate that the Geats had fallen into the habit of relying too much on Beowulf and too little on their own *ellen*—an early example of the demoralizing effects of paternalism. The decision to bury all the dearly won treasure in Beowulf's barrow may have been a magnificent gesture of grief, but it seems to run counter to Beowulf's expressed intention, and it certainly ignores the fact that the treasure could have paid for the hire of many a stout fighter to strengthen the Geats in the perilous days ahead.

BEOWULF'S PRIDE?

After the messenger's speech the people go to look upon Beowulf and the dragon and the treasure from the hoard. Then follows the digression on the spell or curse protecting the hoard (lines 3052–75). Not content with the implication that Beowulf has been guilty of sin or rashness in ordering the plundering of the hoard (lines 3076–81), the author goes on to suggest that Beowulf has been guilty of something like hubris [spiritual pride]. He does, however, put this accusation into the mouth of Wiglaf, who is in the grip of irrational emotion, instead of stating it in his own person. Many must suffer, says Wiglaf, because of the decision of one man. His companions had been unable to persuade Beowulf to let the dragon alone, to let him lie where he had long dwelt until the end of the world.

This is a thoroughly unreasonable speech. The dragon

was not lying quietly in his cave; he was ravaging Beowulf's kingdom, and there is no hint elsewhere in the poem that he had any intent of ceasing to do so. If Beowulf was not to acquiesce supinely [passively] in the destruction of his people, his only choice was one of the means by which he should prevent it. Possibly the author expected his audience to recognize this speech as a mere outburst of feeling. If not, he was inviting more of the same sort of confusion as results from his belated consideration of the curse on the dragon's gold. Perhaps he yielded to the temptation to get every possible theme into the poem. Hubris (*ofermod*) is certainly an accepted theme in Old English poetry, but it is almost as hard to believe that the author would seriously accuse Beowulf of hubris as it is to think that he considered him destined for the bonds of hell. Lines 3050–86 seem to present Beowulf's character in a light so inconsistent with that of the rest of the poem that one leaves them with considerable relief.

THE HEROIC IDEAL

The conclusion, the description of Beowulf's magnificent funeral, is a fitting conclusion to the story of such a hero. . . . The people then build Beowulf's barrow, and twelve warriors ride about it singing his praises: "They said that of the kings of this world he was the mildest and most compassionate of men, kindest to his people and most eager for glory."

Here, not in the confused and confusing passages on curses and hubris, we have the final summing up of Beowulf's character. Commenting on this summary, George Lyman Kittredge observed in his Harvard lectures that it struck a note to match that of the tale of Scyld with which the story opens—a note of exalted resignation. . . . Both kings have done all they can for their people. The worries and lamentations of the living fade into silence in the presence of the mighty dead.

Taken as a whole, the second part of *Beowulf* suffers, like many other sequels, in comparison with the first. A good deal of it appears to be "filler" that could be dispensed with, and lines 3051–85 appear to diverge from the central theme. Nevertheless, it does contribute to the total plan—the presentation of the heroic ideal—for it completes the picture. The young, successful prince becomes the king confronted with an enemy whom he did not seek and over whom he can win only a partial victory. It crowns a heroic life with a heroic death.

BEOWULF'S VALIANT STOICISM

The picture so presented accords with that of the Old English elegy. Happiness and prosperity—all human goods except, perhaps, fame—are transitory. Victories may sometimes be gained, but wars are never really won, and fate stands ever ready to sweep away the lives and works of men. The Christian answer was, of course, to seek the permanent bliss of heaven. The heroic answer, as embodied in *Beowulf,* is a valiant stoicism: "Do your utmost. A good name is all you can win in this world." Very much the same philosophy is summed up in the epitaph (perhaps legendary) of a cowboy: "Here lies Bronco Bill. He always done his damnedest." Angels, it was once observed in a different context, can do no more.

In the light of this philosophy, the "tragedy of the Geats" implicit in Beowulf's death, of which some commentators make a great deal, becomes less significant. All that any man can leave his heirs is a good name and a glorious example. If they cannot be wise and valiant in their own right, he cannot save them. Those who appear to think that if Beowulf could somehow have survived his contest with the dragon both he and the Geats would have survived forever should reread both the poem and history.

The Heroic Standards of Beowulf's World

Michael Swanton

Noted British scholar and translator Michael Swanton explores the heroic values and expectations in *Beowulf.* In contrast to many other scholars, Swanton sees no implied criticism of Beowulf's behavior by the narrator. Beowulf is seen as a model king, though his heroic prowess and acts are ultimately subject to time and fate. To Swanton, Beowulf is both a tragic hero and an epic hero: tragic in that his considerable virtues are insufficient to prevent his defeat, and epic in that the fate of an entire society hinges upon his success or failure.

The *[Beowulf]* poet's theme is the nature of the heroic life— more specifically, the function and character of leadership in heroic society. The didactic content of the poem is high. Even where the poet is not directly moralising, it is easy enough to see the poem advancing through a series of sententiae [wise sayings] culminating in Hrothgar's so-called 'sermon' or 'homily'. In the beginning we are presented with an image of strong Germanic kingship in the person of Scyld Scefing, the founder of his nation's prosperity; in the face of hostile armies, he struck terror into his neighbours, forcing them to pay tribute in submission. This is greeted in terms of unqualified praise: 'that was a great king!' It is the worst possible fate, insists the poet, for a nation to be without a strong king. Subsequently we are shown a son born to Scyld, who by goodness and generosity won the support and loyalty of his people. Among all nations, says the poet, it is only through those actions which merit praise that a man may prosper. This is the key to the heroic ethic: action which leads to glory and praise, *lof* and *dom*, to the attainment of which all men should direct themselves. Life is fleeting: we shall all die; let us therefore so act as to merit the praise and remembrance of men. Scyld's great grandson, Hrothgar, had been a fine example of the heroic king in his youth. Such success in arms and so great a fame attended him, we are told, that kinsmen were eager to serve him, and his *comitatus* [war band] increased in size to a formidable army. . . .

THE HALL AS CENTER OF SOCIETY

It is against this background that we see the introduction of the hall Heorot, the major symbol of the first half of the poem—the integrity of which it is Beowulf's object to preserve. The power of the hall as a poetic image is attested throughout Old English literature; it was the practical and emotional centre of heroic society, all that a man could wish; and its destruction therefore represented the negation of all that society stood for. The symbol of Heorot is introduced with great care by the poet. The home of Hrothgar's people, their source of joy and national harmony, it is shown to be less the palace of a king than the symbol of Denmark as a nation state. It is given a princely name: Heorot; it would be known to occupy a site of extreme sacred antiquity in the Germanic north. At its inauguration there is feasting and music, the universal symbols of order and harmony; the minstrel sings a hymn of creation. And yet at the very moment of its erection we are fore-warned of its eventual destruction. The audience in any case knew very well what the end would be—and Beowulf has not yet entered into his business of saving it from the monsters. The implication is not that his actions are so much futile, as transient. All the glories of mankind are temporary; it is necessary to recognise the reality of this before we can begin to understand the nature of the heroic life.

In his youth, then, Hrothgar had been the type of the ideal Germanic leader, possessed of both wisdom and courage, the mental and physical strength that such a position demands. But while old and full of years, and still the archetypal wise king, Hrothgar now no longer possesses the physical strength he once had. Thus it is that he has need of Beowulf's services. He is not a feeble king: he has had a great career behind him; and it would not be a worthily heroic picture if he were seen to be in any way weak or cowardly. . . . He allows himself to accept Beowulf's offer of assistance, since it merely represents just repayment of help the young Hrothgar had once been able to afford the hero's father in an hour of need. At a time when Hrothgar's physical strength is failing with age, his court apparently falls prey to an external force of disruption. This takes the form of depredation by the monster Grendel, a wretched and unnatural outcast, creature of chaos and outer darkness.

FEAR OF MONSTERS

Early medieval society felt itself closely surrounded by the whole paraphernalia of common pagan fear: hobgoblins, trolls, elves, things that go bump in the night, which dwelt in the wastelands, swamps and deep forests, approaching human awareness only at night, in darkness—and against which the warmth of the hall and its society offered the only security. This belief is not quite so naive as it might at first seem to the average twentieth-century man—who also believes in a whole range of things he has not personally seen, from bacteria to men on the moon, and in literary terms a host of science-fiction wonders. This was not necessarily a belief in the supernatural as such; the poet's trolls and dragons are firmly embedded in a matrix of realism and normality. . . .

Early medieval Europe had no alternative but to externalise its personal and institutional neuroses, and the monster provided a convenient mechanism for fear, then as now. Whatever their origins, physical or mental, it is clear that such monsters represent an evil that could, and should, be encountered and opposed. Not that monsters like Grendel can be defeated once for all; for as the perpetuation of the feud by Grendel's mother demonstrates, the price of freedom is eternal vigilance.

The main outline of Grendel's function within the poem is plain: a creature of darkness and night, outcast by God from the society of men, together with hobgoblins and all other monstrous progenies hostile to human happiness. Associated by the poet with Cain, primordial kinslayer and therefore symbol of elemental social disunity, he stalks abroad, ravaging only by night when the sun . . . is far from the sky. He has made his home with all that is antithetical to Heorot, inhabiting an unvisited land, solitary paths, perilous swamps and the misty wastelands. His lair is a place very like Hell, a dreadful region shunned by all that is good in nature like the noble hart, *heorot*, a major Germanic symbol of both regality and purity. Banished from the society of men, obliged to take the paths of an outcast, he treads the wilderness as an exile, a solitary figure. . . . For heroic society, the solitary figure is invariably suspect and probably vicious, an object of fear and distrust. Although this monster has been proscribed [banished by law] by God, Danish society seems still to be subject to his depredation. He is not effectively banished forever. Haunting the borders of human society, he is always present, neither in nor fully out of it, the corporeal substance of fear, always ready to intrude given opportunity enough. Well known to both the people and the councillors of the king, Grendel and his dam [mother] tread the wastelands in the likeness of men, but misshapen, a mockery of the form of human society, and a public enemy. . . . It is not the physical splendour of Heorot which so angers Grendel, but the order and peace he discerns there. Above all, it is the sweet sound of the harp, archetypal symbol of harmony, that the creature of chaos is unable to bear. . . . Grendel has centred his destructive spite on the heroic society that inhabited the hall Heorot, and apparently without encountering any effective opposition.

THE DEFEAT OF HEOROT

The ancient order seems to have proved ultimately inadequate to oppose such an enemy. Heorot's king, although once a renowned warleader and still both valiant and wise, is now incapable in his own person of bearing the brunt of the attacks. Those to whom he might have looked for support in such a situation, the councillors of his people or his own *comitatus,* both fail him. As with the ancient Swedes or the East Saxons in times of national adversity, war or famine, all the Danish witan [sorceress] can suggest to alleviate public misery is to promise sacrifices at heathen shrines. But this will obviously be of no avail. The poet at least seems well aware of the futility of this course of action. Hrothgar's *comitatus* is no more successful than his witan. Although composed of a great number of noble young warriors like Wulfgar, they are none of them able to put an end to Grendel's encroachments. Asleep in Heorot, grown fat with feasting, they prove all too easy a prey; and the monster has become accustomed to wreak havoc among them, talking up thirty thanes at a time. Despite boasting in their cups the hollowness of heroic Scylding society based on a free *beot* [pledge] is soon apparent, and the *comitatus* dwindles, partly through sheer inactivity and partly through simple lack of courage. The onslaught is so forceful and persistent that the old pattern of free loyalties as represented by the company in Heorot breaks up, and the hall is abandoned. . . .

A NEW KIND OF HERO

The old pattern of loyalties proving unable to contain these new conditions, a new 'kind' of hero is required; and indeed, his reputation has preceded him. Beowulf is already the subject of travellers' tales, a greater man than any other. The introduction of this hero into the decayed Danish kingdom is like the advent of a saviour—a breath of new and vigorous life. He is a stranger to the land, but is immediately recognisable for his plain virtues. Through the eyes of Hrothgar's coast-warden, the hero is seen from the beginning as an essentially active agent, clothed in the fine, bright armour of his business. He is in every way remarkable, singled out from other men as a strong-willed leader. He is a man with a personal sense of mission. His fine war-gear is not merely the affection of pride, but the outward promise of strong action, equipment deserving respect. Arms and armour form a persistent and powerful symbol of heroic activity throughout the poem. And in contrast to the current Danish malaise, this is a man of decisive, strong and vital action who can distinguish between words and deeds. To such a one, the coast-warden recognises, it will be given successfully to survive the hostile encounter. Nevertheless, as Beowulf himself admits, wyrd [fate] will go as it must.

Returning victorious from his second fight against the underwater monsters, the hero concedes that this time his sole strength would have been insufficient without the intervention of Providence, the ruler of victories. He brings with him as proof of his exploit not only Grendel's head, but the hilt of the sword with which the deed was accomplished—and which significantly bears a pictorial allusion to the giants who had warred against God and were thus destroyed in the flood. Hrothgar closely examines the hilt, so eloquent of the ever-present possibility of sudden change in fortune; and it is this he uses as the starting point for his so-called sermon, which forms both the structural and thematic hinge of the poem.

He contrasts Beowulf's virtues with the miserable savagery of the treacherous King Heremod, prophesying the hero's likely accession to power. Beowulf has both strength and wisdom, but must be warned of the cardinal heroic sin of arrogance. Worldly success will often lull the conscience to sleep, and then a hero proves particularly vulnerable to the attacks of evil—and then suddenly, in a variety of ways, death may come upon him—either violently through sword or arrow, or simply through the inevitable decay of old age. Beowulf is therefore urged to take the better part, which is eternal gain—avoiding pride. Only a little while will he be at the height of his powers before old age, disease or the edge of the sword will plunder his strength: its transience is inevitable.

BEOWULF'S LATER CAREER

The second half of the poem might be expected to assess how far the hero lives up to Hrothgar's prophecy of him in face of the inevitable facts of reality. But in fact we are shown very little of his subsequent career, although various allusions hint at such matters as his presence at the death of Hygelac and his role in the Swedish wars. If, as some have supposed, *Beowulf* was intended as a 'mirror for princes', in which young men might encounter in imagination a variety of ennobling situations and thus learn the attitudes appropriate to their place in heroic society, we might have expected the poet to have given full rein to a taste for battle scenes, showing the hero engaged in noble exploits. But there are only oblique allusions to actual physical battles, and the poet seems deliberately to have minimised any battle scene in which the hero might possibly have taken part. Although he has a whole aura of courageous action built round him, the only enemies we see our hero confront are not even human, but incredible monsters and supernatural beings. This then is a curious kind of heroism in some ways. We are soon aware that Beowulf's struggles have broader implications than their outward appearance, involving not merely physical but moral courage. And if there is any moral content, then the conflict with monsters provides a more suitable vehicle than any human battle, however well described, could ever be, simply because the forces of evil are better seen in monstrous shapes. . . .

BEOWULF'S ULTIMATE FAILURE

The end comes about suddenly, almost accidentally. As Hrothgar had warned, one can never tell what change of for-

tune may occur. It is significant that when this trouble comes
to Beowulf—the destruction of his own, like Hrothgar's
court—he is in much the same position the Danish king had
been in when, as a young man, the hero had lent the old king
his strong aid. Beowulf has ruled his kingdom well and
strongly for fifty years—just the length of time that Hrothgar
had reigned—but now he too is old and subject to the weakness of age. But although old, Beowulf is still personally
courageous. His weakness is of a different order from
Hrothgar's inactivity. But the foe that now oppresses his kingdom is of a different order also. Contrary to his usual spirit,
Beowulf falls prey to dismal thoughts. Although no coward,
the hero is no longer resolute and self-confident, now
despairing of God's strength to support his arm. Uneasy and
restless, he gloomily anticipates his doom. . . .

If the great king finally fails, however, there is another
who does not. There comes to him *in extremis,* just as he
himself once came to the aid of the elderly Hrothgar, a
strong prince and heir to his spirit, Wiglaf. His action in join-
ing battle is both an appeal to the heroic code and a recognition of the old king's personal stature. He is certain that,
for as long as Beowulf had ruled the kingdom, he had been
the most honoured hero in the world. And when at last
Wiglaf ignores the express wishes of his leader in coming to
his aid, it was because the old hero did not now deserve to
die alone—if only for the sake of all his past deeds.

But Beowulf's death is merely the climax of the poem.
The tragic denouement is to follow. Now, of course, as
Wiglaf knows, the giving of swords and all the joys of native
land must end, with the dispersal of Beowulf's people into
enforced and despised exile. Whether the entire Geatish
nation was actually annihilated at this point, as some histo-
rians suppose, is immaterial; for the purpose of the narrative
the issue is clear. The messenger who announces the death
of the king to his people serves to confirm both Beowulf's
great *dom* and the dangerous vulnerability of the nation
consequent upon the passing of so strong a ruler. . . .

Nevertheless, whatever may result, no one can deny that
Beowulf had been a great king. As he had wished, his people
erect for him a great barrow high up on Whale's Cape to be
recognised from afar as both a memorial and a landmark for
all those who in future will urge their ships from afar over
the darkness of the seas. The gold, which the hero had died

to win, they again commit to the earth 'as useless to men as it was before'. But the final words of the poem belong to Beowulf's *comitatus*. They declare him to have been the greatest of heroes, of all kings in the world the gentlest and most gracious, kindest to his people and most desirous of renown—one who had truly achieved that *lof* and *dom* for which, as we learned in the beginning, all men should strive.

BOTH TRAGIC AND EPIC HEROISM

Death in some fashion or another must come at last to even the greatest of heroes. Given the ultimate fact of mutability, the Germanic hero is invariably a tragic hero; his virtues are characteristically seen in defence—and often in defeat. But his tragedy has far greater consequences than the merely personal tragedy we associate with the classical or Shakespearian tragic hero. . . .

Beowulf's death has epic implications: it marks the end of a way of life, the destruction of a civilisation. The death of Hector resulted in the fall of Troy. Arthur's death meant the end of the Round Table. Beowulf's death will bring with it the demise of the kingdom of the Geats.

The poet puts into the mouth of the messenger a full awareness of the fate Beowulf had gone so willingly to meet, and which as a result his people will have to meet. In classical tragedy the hero struggles against the fate which some personal tragic flaw has brought about. In this kind of epic literature, however, evil is usually confined to agents external to the hero: Arthur's Mordred or Beowulf's monsters. The epic hero goes willingly to his fate, even though the awful consequences of his choice must be as clear to himself as anyone else. Beowulf dismisses his *comitatus,* but continues to act in the light of the ethical requirements of that group. He believes for an instant—the instant of *beot*—that he *may* overcome the dragon, that he *may* preserve the way of life they all know. The hero defies his fate, but in a spirit of resignation: fate will go always as it must; a man can achieve so much, and no more; he cannot, after all, live forever. His decision may seem to be brought about by pride but, unlike the classical hubris [pride], it is external and clear, not what he but society expects. And whether victorious or defeated, therefore, the end will be that glory, *lof* and *dom,* for which Beowulf, of all men, was the most eager.

The Failure of the Heroic Ideal

Bernard F. Huppé

The ending of *Beowulf* resolves some important issues, but for many readers, it also raises difficult questions. Why did Beowulf insist on fighting the dragon alone? Why are his people going to suffer an unhappy fate? To Bernard F. Huppé, professor emeritus at State University of New York at Binghamton, Beowulf's death represents the spiritual emptiness and inadequacy of the heroic view of life. Beowulf's behavior from beginning to end is governed by the ethic of vengeance and the desire for glory. These attitudes lead to a dismal and inglorious death; for Huppé, Beowulf is trapped in an "iron circle of heroic error."

The epic life of Beowulf unfolds by puzzlement and shadowy recall of the deeds he has done. An ultimate question, however, is not answered. Why does Beowulf, heroically virtuous in death, leave a legacy of worthless gold and a future of unrelieved misery for his people? Although he is the heroic antithesis of Heremod, both leave their people wretched. Why? When Beowulf determines to fight the dragon, why is he filled, not with fear, but with doubt? Why does he have misgivings about transgressing the ancient law when in dying he is aware only of having lived with pious regard to the right uses of the strength given him for destinal purposes? In short, why does the second part of the poem not move to triumphant affirmation of the glory of Beowulf's heroic death, but rather to lamentation over its waste?

These questions, as with Scyld, can only be answered thematically. The answers to them rest in the meaning that is given to the hero's life, and that meaning is based on the poet's concept of the heroic, which, in turn, must reflect a then-current climate of belief. Thus, it would appear essen-

Reprinted, with permission, from Bernard F. Huppé, in *The Hero in the Earthly City*, Medieval & Renaissance Texts & Studies, vol. 33 (Binghamton, NY: MRTS, 1984). Copyright Arizona Board of Regents for Arizona State University.

tial to discover what this attitude was, a seemingly impossible task since the date of *Beowulf* has not been determined. It may have been written during the early, missionary stages of Christianity in England when the triumph of the new religion required apology and vigorous defense (seventh century). It may have been written when Christianity was firmly established and English energies were directed, for example, to the conversion of the continental Saxons (eighth century). Finally, it may have been written after the Viking invasions when English intellectual energies would have been responsive to Scandinavian paganism or, conversely, would have been influenced by Scandinavian Christianity (ninth, tenth, or even eleventh centuries).

All these varying dates, however, belong as a whole to the Christian era when the intellectual life of England was dominated by Augustinian [influenced by St. Augustine, A.D. 354–430] and monastic [from Catholic monasteries] conceptions and constructs. This . . . fact provides the opportunity and governs the attempt to recapture some approximate understanding of the preconceptions . . . that directed the poet's concept of his hero, Beowulf. . . .

A CONFLICT OF IDEALS

Judging from all [the] literary evidence, which spans the entire period in which *Beowulf* could have been written, the heroic tradition appears to have been very much alive, however negatively, in the consciousness of the early medieval poet and writer. Further, the antithesis between heroic and Christian ideals, it must be assumed, presented a primary social problem. . . .

The conflict of ideals would also have presented a basic problem to Christian writers in England from the time of the Conversion until after the Viking invasions. After the Conversion they faced the dilemma of teaching Christianity to an audience brought up with, or vividly remembering, the heroic poetry of the pagan ancestors. . . .

It is tempting to solve this difficulty by resort to the notion that *Beowulf* essentially conveys a pagan heroic ethic which cannot be explained by recourse to the concept of the Christian hero. In such a view the Christian, as merely external coloring, cannot lead to the heart of the poem. Such a solution will not suffice, however, because the Christianity of *Beowulf* has been shown to be an essential part of its form and structure, although its subject and the motivations of its characters are pagan. It would be naive to assume that the poet was not aware of the paganism of his hero and of his society. It would be equally naive to assume that he would have celebrated a society which lacked the knowledge of the truths of Christianity. The values of such a society, lacking in the saving grace of the theological virtues, he would have deplored.

A CHRISTIAN POINT OF VIEW

However, even if a pagan hero were blessed with piety and the cardinal virtues, he could not thereby attain the status of Christian hero. . . .

The epic adventures of a pagan hero can only reveal his limitations and those of his society, for he, without faith, is a blind man leading the blind. Yet this very antithesis between the Christian and pagan understanding of the epic hero provides an hypothesis for the understanding of how *Beowulf* was intended to be read by its Christian audience. The hypothesis assumes that the fictional world of *Beowulf* is pagan, its point of view Christian. From the Christian point of view, the pagan events of the poem reveal the limits of heathen society, the limits of the righteous pagan, and the limits of the heroic ideal. Such Christian revelation is the primary thematic function of the poem.

This hypothesis serves to explain much that is otherwise puzzling in the poem: for one major example, its descending line of mood and action, so that the omens of disaster in the first half of the poem are fulfilled and completed in the last half. After Beowulf returns home and gives his account of his exploits in Denmark, there is a scene of joyous, prosperous amity jarringly concluded without interruption by the twenty-line narrative of ensuing disasters leading to Beowulf's reign, which culminates in the coming of the dragon. Amidst forebodings of disaster, Beowulf decides to revenge the dragon's onslaught and gain the treasure. His mind, however, is darkened by ethical doubt and is filled with memories of past battles. . . .

In the battle [with the dragon], Beowulf is fatally wounded and averts defeat only through the aid of Wiglaf. In his dying speech, Beowulf places his hope for the future upon the gold he has won. His speech, as he gazes upon the gold, recalls in counterpoint the lament of the last survivor as he looked on the useless treasure he was about to bury, a counterpoint of doom and disaster which dominates the last part of the poem. After Beowulf's death the mood is further darkened not so much by grief over his passing as by forebodings of impending doom. The messenger retells the story of Higelac's fatal raid and of the deadly Swedish wars, not to celebrate the hero, but to foretell the disastrous legacy of lordless grief, suffering, and exile that Beowulf will leave to his people.

Further underscoring the dismal view of his death is the contrast between youthful Wiglaf and aged Beowulf. . . .

Beowulf transfers his kingship to Wiglaf who has proved his heroic quality, but Wiglaf does not respond with the assurance of the young Beowulf. He provides no expected show of determination to emulate his dead hero-king; rather he shares completely in the messenger's sense of inevitable disaster. He refuses to share Beowulf's trust in the dragon's treasure, but agrees that it should again be buried to remain as worthless as it was before. Further, he openly declares that Beowulf's encounter with the dragon was the result of a doomed, reckless heroism, a recklessness which will have the ruin of his people as a consequence. . . .

The last words about Beowulf are about his search for glory, the empty ideal of a pagan, heroic world. To the contrary, the poet's attitude toward the heroic ethos and its goal of glory is Christian and critical. That is why the direction of the poem is inevitably toward doom and disaster unrelieved by any sense of hope and redemption. Beowulf's flaw is tragic precisely because there are no means available to him by which the flaw may be redeemed. Thus his tragedy rests in his inability to rise above the ethos of his society, the mores of revenge and war which govern his actions. In the first part of the poem, in contrast to the aged and ineffectual Hrothgar and to the vigorously evil Heremod, Beowulf appears as a savior, a cleanser of evil; in the last part, Beowulf appears to echo and reflect not beginnings but endings. He has become involved in his world and in the ethos of the feud. Though he remains heroic, his heroism is no more effective than is Hrothgar's helplessness. Like Hrothgar he looks toward the past, as does also the last survivor, lamenting the glory that is gone. . . .

TRAPPED BY THE REVENGE CODE

Beowulf, thus introduced, is also an agent of God, as is seen most clearly in his battles against Grendel and particularly against the mother whom he slays with a giant sword to which he is divinely guided. Beowulf brings back the hilt of this sword upon which is recorded the biblical tale of the downfall of the giants, the race of Cain. One effect of the story is to cast Beowulf in the role of God's avenger who eradicates a residue of Cain's generation of monsters. In turn, Hrothgar, gazing on the hilt, is inspired to utter a homily which reaches to the edges of Christian truth. The homily provides a warning to Beowulf against heroic self-reliance whereby his subsequent actions may be judged. Beowulf's own judgment of himself is clouded. On the one hand, when he determines to attack the dragon he is concerned about having violated the old law; on the other hand, in dying he finds comfort in knowing that he has not violated the code by which he has lived. His wavering between moral doubt and certainty results from his being both righteous and pagan. He strives for the truth but cannot escape from the necessary error of all who are without the grace of knowing through faith. Beowulf's striving for righteousness is blocked by the very ethical code which he has piously observed. He cannot understand his feeling that he has transgressed against the old law because he does not know the new law. He has no referent for righteousness except the heroic code, which has revenge as its most sacred obligation, glory and gold as its ultimate reward. The futility of such a code is made evident in Hrethel's fatal ethical dilemma. From the Christian perspective, to seek revenge is sinful error; thus Hrethel, who accepts revenge as ethical obligation, cannot solve his dilemma because he seeks to find his answer in a false faith.

How Beowulf is himself caught in the iron circle of heroic error is evidenced in his inward determination to avenge the death of his nephew, Heardred, Higelac's son, by securing the death of his slayer, Onela, the Swedish king, who had entrusted Beowulf with the Geatish throne, presumably after appropriate swearing of oaths. Beowulf, however, does not perceive that his secret determination to betray Onela is dishonorable because he feels he is being morally obedient to the sacred and paramount duty of revenge. This appears from his dying assertion that he has not dishonored himself with false oaths. Finally, his reasons for attacking the dragon flow from his allegiance to a false moral ideal. He need not have sought revenge; the dragon would have remained in his barrow unless he were again disturbed. For the hero, however, who strives for the ultimate goal of such abiding glory as Sigemund had attained, revenge is an absolute imperative which takes no count of practicalities. Further, the attack on the dragon holds the promise of another ultimate reward, the treasure, visible evidence of glory. In short, as Wiglaf puts it, Beowulf is driven by "relentless doom" because of his own will he seeks the two goals of worldly men living in error, glory and its visible sign, gold. He is doomed because his will now serves a faulty human end. Before, in Denmark, he served as agent of a merciful design, though without understanding; now as king he serves only himself by seeking a heroic goal. In pursuing gold and glory Beowulf becomes the victim of fate because he has accepted the error of his society, and has lost his youthful role as agent of providence.

FUTILITY OF THE HEROIC IDEAL

Thus the final action of the poem takes place not providentially but fatalistically. This fatalism reveals that Beowulf, governed by the law of revenge, is self-doomed, and it reveals the futility of a society not governed and directed by the goal of salvation. The movement of the poem is downward toward a fatally tragic end. Beowulf and the dragon are the victims, the first in seeking the gold, the other in keeping it, and Beowulf's doomed descent is that of all who lack saving grace. The poem ends, to be sure, with Beowulf's people celebrating him as the mildest of kings and the most worthy of praise. He is worthy of praise, however, as the last words of the poem reveal, because he was "most eager for glory." That is, they praise him in terms that would befit any good pagan hero and apply equally well to Aeneas, to Hector, to Odysseus. . . .

Beowulf ends with the death and burial of the hero, which is precisely what might be expected in heroic epic, except that no sense of triumph is imparted. . . .

The first part of the poem reveals and celebrates the workings of God's hand; the death of the hero reveals the emptiness of Beowulf's heroic life when it serves the hero's own ends of glory rather than God's purpose. His death suggests that the heroic ideal is ineffectual and futile, that its supreme embodiment in a Beowulf or an Aeneas lacks any real dignity when compared with the ideal of the

Christian. . . . In this implicit contrast, the tragic implications of Beowulf may most clearly be realized; its pathos rests in the irony of its conclusion where the Geats celebrate a hero who has left them literally nothing but the legacy of debts to be collected.

To conclude, for the author of *Beowulf* and his audience there can be but one ultimate hero, and he is Christ. Whatever is truly heroic comes from the imitation of Him, and the saint is the true hero. . . . Beowulf is a hero who lacks Christ and reveals that the heroic in itself is an empty ideal. The contrast suggests the obvious, that *Beowulf* may have served as Christian apologetic, revealing the error of the ancestral way of the English, however eager for glory it was, and, in contrast, suggesting the truth and validity of Christian faith. Thus a central thematic function of *Beowulf* as Christian apologetic is, through the tragedy of its great and virtuous heathen hero, to promote by antithesis the concept of the Christian hero, true to himself in being true to Christ in seeking not glory but salvation.

The Fatal Contradiction in *Beowulf*

John D. Niles

In this essay, noted *Beowulf* scholar John D. Niles
argues that the heroic code of Beowulf is both
admirable and practical. Niles, a professor of English
at the University of California, Berkeley, contends that
no tragic flaw can be found in either Beowulf or the
values of his society. He suggests that if blame must
be assigned for a disintegrating society, it should go to
those around Beowulf for failing to live up to the
heroic code as Beowulf does. Niles holds that, far
from acting selfishly, Beowulf consistently acts for the
good of his people, as a good king should.

Early readers of *Beowulf* seem to have been untroubled by
suspicions that the poem's surface simplicity is undercut by
moral ambiguities. Scholars assumed with some unanimity
that the hero's life is intended to exemplify qualities deemed
worthy of imitation in the kind of society that the poem
describes and, presumably, from which it came. [Frederick]
Klaeber refers to Beowulf as a "warrior brave and gentle,
blameless in thought and deed," for example, a "singularly
spotless hero" who in the end "dies for his people.". . .

During the past thirty years or so, readings of *Beowulf* have
been proposed that depart so profoundly from such assumptions that one wonders if the same poem is being discussed. The
hero has been seen [by W.F. Bolton] as a "benighted pagan" who
capitulates to his desire for the gold and is damned. His entire
life has been seen [by Larry D. Benson] as "a falling off from . . .
one moment of triumph," the Grendel fight, so that in the end
he meets with "utter defeat" and dies "in vain." At best, the heroic ideal that motivates the hero's behavior is seen [by Barbara
Raw] as something "splendid but impractical" that does not, in
the end, bear imitating.

Such disagreements concerning the core issues of the poem not only reflect a restless discomfort with easy answers, they suggest the rough interpretive parameters within which the text may have functioned from the beginning. The original audience of *Beowulf* is not likely to have been uniform in either social standing or values. It may have included thanes [warriors] and monks, men and women, noblemen and commoners, young and old. Not only modern readers have a right to disagree about the meaning of a literary work from the past. From an early time, the work may have meant different things to different listeners. . . .

My remarks might seem to be leading to the conclusion that those who praise the hero and those who damn him are equally justified, given the possibility of medieval precedent for either view. This is not my point. . . . While ultimately an author's intentions may be irrecoverable, the text is not lost, and one can tell what it says, always allowing for the possibility of honest disagreement about the meaning of certain words and phrases.

In my own view, *Beowulf* expresses an essentially conservative impulse. First and foremost, it praises a life lived in accord with ideals that help perpetuate the best features of the kind of society it depicts. The ideals deserve the name "heroic," but they are of Christian and well-nigh universal significance as well. Most notably they include the notions of unflinching courage in the face of adversity; unswerving loyalty in fulfilling one's duty to one's king, one's kindred, and one's word, and in carrying out one's earned or inherited social obligations in general; and unsparing generosity, particularly on the part of kings and queens. While these ideals motivate the conduct of many people in the poem, they find most consistent expression in the life of Beowulf, who is depicted at various stages of life and whose great adventures successively exemplify praiseworthy conduct in a young warrior and an aged king. The heroic code by which Beowulf lives is not presented as something splendid and impractical, but as splendid and eminently *practical* in that societies are shown to stand or fall in accord with their ability to sustain it.

THE ARGUMENTS CRITICIZING BEOWULF'S HEROISM

In a pivotal article published in 1965 under the title "Beowulf the Hero and the King," John Leyerle sets forth a series of judgments that, while never before voiced, have been accepted in much subsequent criticism and that effectively undermine the value of the hero's self-sacrificing death. In Leyerle's view, "The poem presents a criticism of the essential weakness of the society it portrays." Its major theme is not individual heroism but "the fatal contradiction at the core of heroic society":

> The hero follows a code that exalts indomitable will and valour in the individual, but society requires a king who acts for the common good, not for his own glory. The greater the hero, the more likely his tendency to imprudent action as king. The three battles with the monsters, the central episodes in the poem, reveal a pattern in which Beowulf's preeminence as a hero leads to the destruction of the Geats when he becomes king. . . .

While such a point of view is foreshadowed in [J.R.R.] Tolkien's mistranslation of the poem's last word, *lofgeornost* ("most eager for praise"), as "too eager for praise," Leyerle goes beyond Tolkien in developing a comprehensive theory of the poem based on the notion of the hero's faults. Among critics who have accepted the theory is Margaret E. Goldsmith, who has sought to distinguish the good hero of part I of the poem from the flawed hero of part II. In her view, which goes beyond Leyerle's in its emphasis on the poem's religiosity, the aged Beowulf suffers from "the spiritual deterioration described by Hrothgar." In the end, the king's pride and self-will lead not only to his own death but to the destruction of his people. According to this reasoning, the hero, by being heroic, fails to fulfill his proper duties as king. . . .

Such negative verdicts concerning the value of the hero's final self-sacrifice maintain an appeal whose attractiveness is chiefly a priori [presumed] rather than based on the text. . . .

All in all, however, the mood of gloom is tempered by exultation. Any incidental or unspoken criticism of the hero is far outweighed by emphatic praise, while the "fatal contradiction at the core of heroic society" boils down to no more than the recognition that the kind of action that holds society together in times of crisis is not met with frequently, hence human life in general tends to be unstable. To justify this view, let me take up, one by one, the key questions on which a judgment of the hero's actions must be based.

Is Beowulf's Decision to Fight the Dragon Imprudent?

Many critics say yes: the dragon should have been left alone. This is Wiglaf's wisdom, as expressed in a speech that some

readers take as the poet's final word on the question of the
hero's prudence. . . .

> Often must many men   suffer misery
> through one man's will   as has happened with us.
> We could not give   our beloved ruler,
> shepherd of the realm,   any advice
> not to seek out   the guard of the gold
> but let him be   where he long had lain
> dwelling at home   till the world's end.
> He kept to his high destiny. . . .

Although the gist of Wiglaf's speech is clear, its details are
fraught with uncertainties, and the translation I have offered
must be taken as tentative.

First, does *anes willan* mean "through one man's will," or
"for the sake of one [person]," as Klaeber glosses the words?
If the latter, Wiglaf means only that the Geats are lamenting
Beowulf's death; if the former, he means to say that
Beowulf's stubborn decision to fight the dragon led to their
misery. Grammar will not determine the matter. Given the
speaker's emphasis in the next lines on the hero's refusal to
accept any moderating advice, however, I discern a note of
criticism as well as regret in Wiglaf's words. . . .

These questions of words and their meaning do not
resolve a more general question. Why are we told only at
this point, after the fight, that the hero went against the
advice of his counselors? The poet's practice here calls to
mind an earlier passage when, long after the fact, Hygelac
mentions to Beowulf that he had opposed the hero's journey
to Denmark. In that prior instance the introduction of the
motif of "stubborn action against contrary advice" served to
raise the hero in the estimation of the audience by showing
how he achieved his victory in spite of timid counsel. Here
much the same end is achieved, for Beowulf has won even
greater glory than before. Even while dwelling on the cost of
the king's achievement, Wiglaf pays tribute to the man who
alone "kept to his high destiny" when his countrymen were
urging him to evade it. A wholly different effect would have
resulted had the poet chronologically shown first the dragon's attack, then the counselors' advice to the king, then
Beowulf's defiance of this advice. . . .

Wiglaf's speech raises still another question. Can one
assume, with the counselors, that the dragon was going to lie
quiet in its barrow "till the world's end"? If so, then they were
right, and Beowulf's contrary decision to counterattack was

the height of folly. Unfortunately the poet does not specify the dragon's intentions. Perhaps the counselors were right; perhaps they engaged in wishful thinking. All one knows is that the dragon burned down the Geats' stronghold and fully intended to leave nothing alive. Because it has already tried to do this once, Beowulf scarcely seems rash in seeking to prevent it from making a renewed attack. In a crisis like this, taking action can be more prudent than hiding one's head in the sand. Hrothgar responded passively to Grendel's threat, and his troubles continued for twelve years. As *folces weard*, "guardian of the tribe," Beowulf is aware of his responsibility to exercise leadership. He still possesses the cup whose theft, as he now knows, incited the dragon's ire. He has no way of knowing whether or not this ire has ceased, and so, with little hesitation, he offers his own life in exchange for the dragon's. His people therefore honor him "as is proper" for what the narrator calls his "courageous deed", and there is no reason why critics should fail to do the same.

SHOULD THE HERO HAVE ACCEPTED HELP?

Here interpretation seems to be on solid ground. According to every dictate of military science, the king was foolish not to have surrounded himself with able warriors once he had reached his decision, so that he could fight with the most chance for success. His choice of single combat seems an act of arrogance based on a serious underestimation of the dragon's power. The key lines are 2345-50:

Then the lord of rings   scorned to seek out
that far-flier   with a troop of men,
an ample host;   he did not fear the fight
or value in the least   the dragon's power
or strength in battle   because he earlier had come
through many a combat   taking dire risks. . . .

If Beowulf did not worry about the dragon's power, he was foolish. The dragon itself settles this question. If Wiglaf had not come to offer help, the king would have died in the dragon's jaws without ever having killed it.

Yet the matter is not so simple. To what extent should the hero be blamed for not counting on the help of people who were opposed to the fight in the first place, as Wiglaf later tells us the Geats were? Even the hand-picked companions whom Beowulf had stationed near the barrow turn and run for the woods as soon as the dragon gives a good snort. Of these eleven men, presumably those with the closest ties of duty to their king, only Wiglaf turns out to be of the least use, and he is an untried warrior. Leaving aside his extraordinary act of courage, which even Wiglaf admits went *ofer min gemet*, "beyond my normal power," Beowulf takes the measure of his men with realism unclouded by false hopes. They even betray the little faith he puts in them. If he had depended on their direct support, his situation would have been still more desperate. When he excludes them from direct participation in the fight with the words, "That is not your business, nor is any man suited for it except myself," he is expressing, without false modesty, the unfortunate truth.

In addition, the narrator's statement that Beowulf did not fear the fight or respect the dragon's power cannot be accepted without qualification, for to a certain extent these words are contradicted by statements elsewhere. If the hero truly expected no trouble in the fight, he would not have made special preparations for it by forging an iron shield. . . .

The king's courage in the face of his probable death is of course commendable, and it is what permits him to kill his enemy. His supposed underestimation of the dragon's power is counterweighed by signs of his awareness that any victory could not be achieved lightly. As Beowulf sets out for the barrow, the poet therefore does not condemn him for making light of the encounter but praises him for undertaking it despite its known risks. "He trusted in his solitary strength," the poet says, and adds, "that is no coward's way!"

DOES THE HERO ACT FOR HIS OWN GLORY, OUT OF PRIDE?

By calling the hero's pride "understandable, almost inevitable," one is freed from the constraint of having to show evidence that it exists—exists in the sense of "arrogance," that is, for a certain amount of pride can be a good thing. It can keep a person like Wiglaf from running for the woods, for example, when others are doing so. The chief question is whether the king's motive was a desire for personal glory rather than the common good. . . .

Nothing in the fight suggests that the king enters it as a way of winning personal glory rather than as (in [G.N.] Garmonsway's well-chosen words) "a moral act which his honor compels him to undertake." Before the fight he declares himself willing to accept whatever outcome the Lord sees fit to grant. Afterward he gives thanks to "the Lord

REVENGE IS GOOD IN *BEOWULF*

Though we may not agree with a code of ethics based on the idea of revenge, Beowulf *scholar John M. Hill asserts that this ethic is endorsed in* Beowulf. *This excerpt is taken from Hill's recent book* The Cultural World in Beowulf.

As for revenge and feud, *Beowulf* scholarship reflects a nearly settled view that the poem implicitly undermines the ethic of revenge by showing how vicious, interminable, and destructive it becomes—all kingdoms suffer through hard times or simply come to grief. Yet Beowulf himself announces the good of revenge. Hrothgar rejoices in the prospect of it, and God effectually underwrites it as an honourable action—note the revenge He takes upon giants and Grendel and his favour on Beowulf's behalf. . . . We are not to say that revenge is awful but rather we are asked to consider the vicissitudes of a violent world.

of all, the King of glory, eternal God" for having been "permitted"—the phrasing is again significant because it reflects the king's respect for the source of his fortune—to gain such a magnificent hoard for his people. He does not exult in the hoard for himself, for he will have no need of it. He rejoices in having won great treasure for his people as an incidental outcome of having killed the dragon, and he urges Wiglaf to continue to act for the need of the tribe. He reviews the conduct of his past life without regrets, for he has kept the peace, has not sought out trouble, has not sworn false oaths, has not persecuted his kinsmen, and in general has refrained from the type of behavior that Hrothgar had warned him against with reference to Heremod. At the same time, he refrains from exulting in his personal riches or achievements, and his last words are a model of restraint. . . .

[Beowulf] conducts himself with the dignity that one expects of persons of rank. . . . He rules with strength and with a constant regard for the needs of his people. When he dies, he thus meets the judgment that awaits the righteous, while his people praise his kindness above all his other virtues.

IS THE HERO DEFEATED, AND DOES HE DIE IN VAIN?

Despite the contrary opinions of others, I fail to see how Beowulf can be considered to meet with "utter defeat" at the end of his life in a "losing battle against the evil powers" when he accomplishes what he had set out to do. The cost of his success is high, from one point of view, but he and Wiglaf succeed in killing an enemy that had visited the Geats with unparalleled destruction and that posed a continuing threat. He wins a magnificent hoard for his people, they suffer not a single casualty, and he is able to accomplish these things while living up to his pledge not to flee one foot from the barrow. If the narrator had meant us to consider the fight a defeat, it is hard to see why he refers to it as the hero's "last triumph" and speaks of Wiglaf as "exultant in victory.". . .

The winning of the treasure skirts the main issue, however, which is the fate of the Geats. Does Beowulf's preeminence as a hero lead to the ruin of his tribe when he becomes king, as is claimed by Leyerle? Does his recklessness destroy the Geats, as Goldsmith holds? These charges are serious but unfounded. On the contrary, his preeminence as a hero leads to fifty years of peace when he becomes king. The poet tells us this fact once and Beowulf himself speaks of it with some pride later on. He adds that not a single neighboring king dared attack him during this period, while he never sought out a fight himself. . . .

The magnitude of Beowulf's accomplishment as king of the Geats is not to be taken lightly, even though the poet does not choose to make a great issue of these years of peace. After all, peace is not a promising subject for a heroic poem. One should not judge his success by the events of a single last day.

Even on this day, if his conduct were such as to destroy his people one would have to judge him severely, but he does not cause the troubles that the Geats are soon to suffer. They bring these troubles on themselves. The poet makes this point clear in Wiglaf's speech to the ten cowardly Geats, when they emerge from the woods "shame-faced" to face his tongue-lashing. . . .

He singles out the Geats' cowardice, not their hero's death, as the source of their approaching misfortunes. Those who condemn the king for dying seem to assume that he was going to live forever. The important question is: Will the king leave behind him leaders capable of defending the realm with courage and strength like his? The Geats have provided a visible answer to this question by running away. . . .

No Tragic Flaw in Beowulf

If the behavior of anyone in the poem is to be considered irresponsible and impractical, it is that of the Geats, whose failure to live by the heroic ideal proves to be impractical in the extreme, even to the point of leading to their ruin as soon as they no longer have a hero to protect them. Rather than suffering spiritual deterioration, Beowulf ends his mature life as he had begun it years before in Hrothgar's court, with acts of splendid and uncompromising devotion to a code of conduct that places the good of others above oneself. Of all the persons in the poem it is he who most commands admiration, for he wins not only fame for his personal heroism and salvation for a life lived justly, but the name of a good king for having directed his energies for the welfare of society rather than for his own advantage.

There is thus no need to look for a tragic flaw in either the hero or his society. In this poem, as has been wisely remarked, "the tragic element is built into the very fabric of life itself and is as natural as the coming of spring or of a dragon." As for the hero's death, without perhaps being a "triumph" it can hardly be considered a defeat that indicates that his actions were foolish or that he had somehow fallen from grace. As one critic has put it, "That sinners live and saints die is a fact of every-day experience which does not prove that God is with the former and against the latter." Beowulf went into battle fully cognizant that he might die, and the prospect did not make him cringe. He shows a Christian readiness for death and an awareness that all things are in divine dispensation. His last words express neither regret nor self-incrimination, but only a quiet satisfaction that he has accomplished what he set out to do.

Does the poem then present "a criticism of the essential weakness of the society it portrays"? In a certain way, yes: not by showing how a decision to act by the heroic ideal can lead to disaster, but by showing how a failure to act by the heroic ideal can do so. If the society portrayed in *Beowulf* is weak, its weakness can be ascribed to the too-frequent failure of people to live by the ethics that, when put into practice, hold society together. The fatal contradiction developed through the narrative of *Beowulf* is nothing inherent in heroic society, feudal society, capitalist or Marxist society, or any other social system. It is lodged within the recalcitrant breasts of human beings who in times of crisis find themselves unable to live up to the ideals to which their lips give assent. The poem does not criticize the hero for being unlike the Geats. It criticizes all of us for not being more like the hero.

CHAPTER 3

Thematic and Structural Issues in *Beowulf*

The Struggle Between Order and Chaos in *Beowulf*

John Halverson

The fragility and instability of Anglo-Saxon society are very evident in *Beowulf:* Both the Danish hall Heorot and Beowulf's own hall are destroyed, and the people of those halls are scattered. In the following essay, University of California, Santa Cruz, scholar John Halverson describes the yearning for order and stability in *Beowulf* as a central theme of the poem. Halverson contends that the poem blames the rampant individualism of the people and their unwillingness to act for the common good for the downfall of the societies depicted in *Beowulf.*

In the first part of *Beowulf,* Heorot is the center of the world. Almost all movement is focused on it. Grendel seeks it out for destructive purposes; Beowulf comes to cleanse it. All the nobles assemble there; there the King presides and distributes treasure. It shines out over many lands, a beacon of civilization; it is the people's place. For the dwellers on earth it is the foremost building under the heavens. It towers, "greatest of halls," spacious and gold-adorned, on a high place. Lavishly adorned, it is a splendid, shining structure. It is the work of many hands; many a people is called upon to decorate the people's place: it is the product of social enterprise. It is a place of protection, a place of safety, above all, a place of communal joy, of light, warmth, song, and companionship. The festivities of the hall are suffused with the social pleasures of food and drink and the music of the harp. The queen, adorned with gold, moves among the people, greets them, proffers a cup. There is always the pleasant sound of human voices. . . .

The hall is where treasure is distributed, a function uppermost in Hrothgar's mind when he builds Heorot. "Nor

Reprinted by permission of The Johns Hopkins University Press from "The World of *Beowulf,*" by John Halverson, *ELH,* vol. 36, no. 4, December 1969, pp. 593–608. Copyright © 1969 by The Johns Hopkins Press.

did he belie that promise; he distributed bracelets, treasure at the feast.". . . Heorot is not only a monumental artifact, an achievement of *homo faber* [man the maker]; it is also the center for *homo politicus* [political man], the place of social joy, music, drinking and feasting, the source of pleasure, where friends and kinsmen are together in peace. The hall embodies all the good things of this world; it represents the principle of harmony: everything is in order. . . .

THE HOSTILE OUTSIDE WORLD

There are in *Beowulf* numerous references to, and some detailed description of, artifacts, particularly treasure. . . . In comparison there is notably little description of nature. What there is is mostly associated with the monsters of the poem, and presents the outside world as cold, dark, and forbidding. We hear often of windy nesses, wastelands, fens, dark and hidden places, and the stormy sea, but rarely of "glory-bright weather" or "lush fields fair." The most compelling and famous descriptions are of the haunts of Grendel and his dam, and of the stormy sea in the Breca episode. When the natural world is the poet's subject, the emphasis is usually on its grimmer and more hostile aspects: night, coldness, storm, waste. In general it is alien to the people, whose pleasures are associated with the hall, shut off from the world out there. The pleasures of the outdoors are not unknown, but they have no significant part in the poem. The social world, the civilized world, is distinctly inside.

The hostility of the natural world and its inherently antisocial aspects are embodied in Grendel. He is above all a creature of the night, a walker of the darkness, he who bides in darkness and the black nights; he is the greatest of the night's evils. All of his destructive actions are perpetrated at night; during the day Hrothgar and his court safely occupy Heorot. Grendel dwells in the wasteland, the fens and moors. . . .

He is not only alone, he is alien, an "ellorgast," a spirit from elsewhere, as is his mother. He is deprived of joy like his progenitor Cain, who fled the joys of men and dwelled in the wasteland. . . . Grendel's abode is a "joyless den"; the mere is in a joyless wood. Moreover, he hates the joys of men. . . .

It is the great hall with its sound of human conviviality that vexes this monster of the outer darkness and rouses him to terrible action. He is called enemy of the Danes and of

Hrothgar and he surely is, but Heorot itself is the target of his attacks, for Heorot embodies the achievement of civilization; its size, appearance and prominence seem to flaunt that achievement in the face of a hostile world. It enrages Grendel, who, living in solitude, darkness and silence and knowing no joy, embodies the "fearsome world outside.". . .

CONFLICTING WORLDS

The contrast and conflict of two worlds—inside and outside, the world of man and the world of monsters, the world of order and the world of chaos—constitute the basic philosophical and psychological structure of *Beowulf.* On one side is the world enclosed by the walls of Heorot and presided over by Hrothgar. It is a man-made world, its construction requiring cooperative labor, art and technology; in it men speak and act rationally and according to custom; there is about it a sense of material and social form. It is a world that represents the imposition of order and organization on chaotic surroundings. The results of this ordering are (temporarily) security, light and warmth. It is a socially collective world, where the pleasures of human companionship can be enjoyed in the feasting and drinking, in the sharing of treasure, in talking, in the playing of the harp and the reciting of old tales.

The world out there—cold, dark, and cheerless—is dominated by the image of fens and moors haunted by the two monsters, solitary creatures who cannot participate in the joy of the community and who savagely hate its existence. As Hrothgar is a maker, they are destroyers. Because their world is without form, it is without security and without pleasure. It is silent, frightening, monstrous. This is the world represented by the mere when the heralding blast of the trumpet disturbs its watery silence, maddening the monster serpents, who can bear the sound of the horn no more than Grendel the sound of harps.

This polar opposition of worlds is so fundamental that it gives an inevitable, fatal quality to the critical conflict of *Beowulf,* the struggle between the civilized world and the world out there, which begins with the invasion of Heorot by Grendel. No reason is given for Grendel's rage against Heorot; it is sudden, gratuitous, and irrational. It would seem (though it is not an obligatory inference) that Grendel has been around for some time; it is the building of Heorot that enrages him and goads him to his depredations. Precisely directed and motivated, his attack is not against the Danes as such but against the great hall, or rather what the hall stands for and makes possible: the establishment of human order with its consequent pleasures. Though he rejoices in slaughter as he goes to seek his dwelling, still his motive is not simply dietary, for apparently everyone stays out of Heorot after dark, which seems all that is required to avoid being eaten. Presumably Grendel could find his victims someplace besides Heorot, but he doesn't. His essential purpose, then, must be what in fact he accomplishes: he empties the hall. He breaks down the doors to this little enclosed world, puts out the light, lets in the cold, and, himself the embodiment of chaos, presides in darkness over Heorot, the construct of order.

So too Hrothgar's constant affliction and woe over twelve years seem to be due as much to this fact as to actual loss of life. His great achievements are being negated by the monster, and not only the Danes suffer but the precarious status of civilization as well. The resolution of this impasse, the "bright remedy" of which the Danes despair, comes from across the sea.

THE DEFENDER OF CIVILIZATION

When Beowulf hears of Hrothgar's peril, he takes no thought of his action, but responds instantly. It is his natural function, as it were, to restore order where it has been upset. The Danes are otherwise nothing to him. Heorot is polluted, the once bright center plunged into darkness, the enclosure of civilization broken down. The atmosphere of the land of the Danes is one of gloom, hopelessness, and stasis; Danish society has been rendered immobile and desperate. In sharpest contrast to this murky atmosphere, the introduction of Beowulf into the poem is accompanied by the flash and rattle of armor, the fresh sea air, the bustle of activity; all that Beowulf and his men do is alive with purpose, direction and hope. . . . Beowulf's first announced goal is to seek out the war-king over the sea, and his progress is single-mindedly in that direction, straight to the king, and when he is at last in the king's presence, he comes instantly to the point. He has heard of the Grendel affair; he would cleanse Heorot. Again the hall is the center of the narrative structure. Beowulf's role is that of civilization's champion, the hero who restores order when it has been weakened or destroyed. What is wrong in Denmark is not so much that Grendel terrifies the people but that the great hall stands "useless and deserted." When Beowulf finally succeeds in destroying the monsters, Heorot once more becomes the center of warmth, light and companionship, and the hero's mission is accomplished.

In the last part of the poem, Beowulf's role is much the same, and the situations and incidents are also parallel to those of the first part. The crisis which the hero is called upon to deal with is the depredation of a solitary monster of the night, now a dragon. . . . Like Grendel, the dragon hates and humiliates men. Like Grendel, the dragon directs his wrath at the dwellings of men, and his terrors are known far and wide. To Beowulf, again, the crisis is made known. His own hall . . . is consumed by fire. And like Hrothgar, he is filled with sorrow. But as he had done in the past, he acts instantly and purposefully.

The pattern of significant events is quite like that of the first part. A monster of the night who embodies all that is hostile and terrifying about the world out there threatens to annihilate the constructed human world of "bright houses." The hero, responding to this crisis with speed and purpose, assumes the role of defender and restorer of civilization. The significant difference is in the outcome of the hero's battle, for in his final struggle against the destructive forces of the world outside, Beowulf is himself destroyed.

FEAR OF ULTIMATE DESTRUCTION

The result of the conflict between the constructed, rationalized human world and the chaotic, frightening world out there is not reassuring. The victories of Beowulf are great ones, but they are temporary; the threat remains, and the entire poem is haunted by the vision of ultimate destruction. The life of man and the works of man are fleeting and doomed. The Christian consolation of salvation has no significant part in *Beowulf.* . . .

The work of man *par excellence* is Heorot, and in one breath the poet describes its construction and anticipates its ruin. . . .

Beowulf, Hrothgar, Heorot, the achievements of civilization constitute a brave and defiant intrusion of human order into the formlessness of the outside world. But it is a doomed enterprise, for more than a temporary establishment is as yet beyond the capacity of the struggling society represented by the poem. . . .

In the earlier period, it is hardly necessary to demonstrate the wretched and precarious state of civilization. As for the eighth-century English background, much as may be said admiringly of the cultural efflorescences of Northumbria and Mercia, their "brilliance" is highly relative. The age of Bede and Boniface was also the age of Æthelbald, barbarian and dissolute tyrant, murdered by his own bodyguard. The learning of the period was a matter of Latin scholarship and theological commentary, not knowledge of the external world. The evidence of the gnomic [proverbial] sayings, spells, saints' lives and the chronicles points to a prevalence of credulousness and superstition and fear. How could it be otherwise? Every burgeoning of civilized life had to contend not only with the encroachment and resistance of nature but also with human destructiveness. It was an age of violence. Boniface was murdered by heathens. Bede's monastery, and the entire northern culture, were annihilated in a moment. It would be surprising, under such circumstances, to find much optimism about the durability of the works of man or much skepticism about the supernatural.

The pathos of much Old English poetry, especially *Beowulf*, is based on themes of isolation, exile, and the dissolution of social order. The prophecies at the end of *Beowulf* concern the break-up of Geatish society. There is a recurring sense of yearning for social stability and material durability: a dynasty that will not be destroyed by feud and war, a hall that will not be consumed by fire or ravaged by monsters. . . .

LOYALTY TO THE INDIVIDUAL

The Dark Ages period is an heroic age, the time of the individual hero. Everything depends on "the will of one man." In the west, the order and culture of civilization are moments of history associated with single powerful men: Clovis, Offa, Penda, Charlemagne, Alfred. Their kingdoms rise, flourish briefly, and decline with the deaths of their creators. When we speak of civilization in this period, we speak of one or two generations only. It is the great men who, by force of personality and military capacity, alone keep together the fabric of civilization, and when they die the order they have established soon disintegrates. Inevitably perhaps, for the kingdom is an extension of a personality, the king an exten-

JOY IN THE MEAD HALL

A number of scholars have noted the centrality of the hall and its symbolism in Beowulf. *In this excerpt from his book* Images of Community in Old English Poetry, *scholar Hugh Magennis describes the communal and spiritual joy in Heorot that so aggravates Grendel.*

Grendel is incited to attack Heorot in the first place because of his hostility to the civilization which it represents and epitomizes. In particular, the song of the *scop* [singer], mentioned in the context of joy in the hall, enrages him: he finds it hard to bear "that every day he heard joy loud in the hall; there was the sound of the harp, the clear song of the *scop* (88–90). Hall-joy, the communal, civilized life of humankind, is what angers Grendel. And the song which he hears and which suggests this communal life combines the connotations of Germanic society with a distinctly biblical-sounding content. The *scop* sings, Cædmon-like, of God's creation of the world: God made the plain of the earth and the sea which surrounds it, he made the sun and the moon for the benefit of humankind, and he created all living things. This song, as well as signifying the joy of the Danes, represents an awareness and acceptance on their part of the goodness of God. Thus in the song of the *scop*, sung in praise of and in harmony with the goodness of God, there is a fusion of spiritual and communal values, which in his profound evil Grendel cannot tolerate. The religious content of the song intensifies the sense of good associated with Heorot and reinforces the symbolic importance of hall and feasting imagery in the poem.

sion of the father. He carves out a patrimony, the realm is private property. But durable order depends on depersonalization, that is, on the establishment of institutions; and the Dark Ages suffer from an excess of individualism. In an altogether personalistic era, the center of order is conceivable only as a person. One cannot yet say, "The king is dead, long live the king," but only, "Beowulf is dead—what will happen now?" The abstractions "king," "state" have not yet taken on a life of their own.

Old English poetry is infused with a sense of mortality and mutability. There was no lack of awareness that life is short and hard. But there is also, as a kind of compensation, a naive cherishing of artifacts: the old treasures that survive through time and can be handed down across the generations. The supreme artifact is the house of man, Heorot, where the world's vicissitudes are transcended in a moment of human collectivity. But it is a dream. The monsters of the night invade the hall, the dragon seizes the treasure. If the hero restores the hall and treasure, it is only for the moment, for his time.

Men had learned to create order, but not how to make it last. The only way to do that is by common effort. The church had the vision of a united Christendom, but no independent capacity to realize it. . . . Secular society, however, was taking the first steps towards such a goal in the extension of kinship loyalties to larger groups, the beginnings of feudal contractualism. One of the weaknesses of early feudalism comes from its source in the family: it remains personal and individual; loyalty is owed to a man, not to an office or institution.

The code of loyalty, personal or impersonal, is implicitly and potentially a means toward social unity; it expresses the intent of cooperation. Why does it fail? Because of individualism. The "cowardice" of the retainers is simply an expression of the priority of the individual over the group. Wiglaf seems dimly to see the dilemma, the glory and the curse of individualism. The retainers were not legally culpable for not coming to Beowulf's aid; they did only what they were told to do. Yet Wiglaf's denunciation and his evocation of the loyalty code are right, for the saving of their society requires the cooperative effort that the code contemplates. He also sees the limitations of individual heroism. Beowulf, the greatest of heroes, is loved and revered by his nephew, but the heroic solution is not always the best solution. It is not Beowulf's pride that brings about the ultimate catastrophe, but precisely his heroism. He is not a victim of ego inflation; he simply cannot see other alternatives to his own way. He is a victim of the heroic milieu; he is molded gloriously and inflexibly by his world.

Grendel's Mother and the Women of *Beowulf*

Jane Chance

The role of the women in *Beowulf* has long been debated; are they primarily active participants in the life of the hall or passive victims of the behavior of the men? Jane Chance, a professor of English at Rice University, argues that the character of Grendel's mother provides the best focus for assessing the representations of women in the poem. Chance contends that the human women are primarily passive sufferers of male violence, but that Grendel's mother provides an alternative view of the female as actively seeking to rectify or revenge the wrongs she has suffered.

The episode in *Beowulf* involving Grendel's mother has been viewed as largely extraneous, a blot upon the thematic and structural unity of the poem. If the poem is regarded as two-part in structure, balancing contrasts between the hero's youth and old age, his rise as a retainer and his fall as a king, his battles with the Grendel family and his battle with the dragon, then her episode (which includes Hrothgar's sermon and Hygelac's welcoming court celebration with its recapitulation of earlier events) lengthens the first "half" focusing on his youth to two-thirds of the poem (lines 1–2199). If the poem is regarded as three-part in structure, with each part centering on one of the three monsters or the three fights, then the brevity of her episode again mars the structural balance: . . . Even if her episode is lengthened to a thousand lines so as to include Hrothgar's sermon and Hygelac's court celebration, still Grendel's mother hardly dominates these events literally or symbolically as do Grendel and the dragon the events in their sections.

But her battle with Beowulf (and this middle section of the poem) is more than merely a "transition between two

Reprinted from Jane Chance Nitzsche, "The Structural Unity of *Beowulf*: The Problem of Grendel's Mother," *Texas Studies in Literature and Language*, vol. 22, no. 3, Fall 1980, pp. 287–303, by permission of the author and the University of Texas Press.

great crises," even though it is "linked with both the Grendel fight and the Dragon fight" [Adrien Bonjour]. The key to her significance may indeed derive from her links with the other two monsters. . . .

THE INVERSION OF FEMININE IDEALS

Like these monsters, Grendel's mother is also described in human and social terms. She is specifically called a "monstrous woman" and a "lady monster-woman.". . . It seems clear from these epithets that Grendel's mother inverts the Germanic roles of the mother and queen, or lady. She has the form of a woman and is weaker than a man and more cowardly, for she flees in fear for her life when discovered in Heorot. But unlike most mothers and queens, she fights her own battles. *Maxims* I testifies that, "Battle, war, must develop in the man, and the woman must flourish beloved among her people, must be light-hearted."

Because the poet wishes to stress this specific inversion of the Anglo-Saxon ideal of woman as both monstrous and masculine he labels her domain a "battle-hall.". . .

The poet constantly contrasts the unnatural behavior of Grendel's dam with that of the feminine ideal by presenting human examples as foils in each of the two parts. We turn first to an examination of the female ideal in *Beowulf,* then to a detailed analysis of the episode involving Grendel's mother and its two parts, and finally to some conclusions regarding the structural unity of the entire poem.

THE WOMAN AS PEACE-WEAVER

The role of woman in *Beowulf* primarily depends upon "peace-making," either biologically through her marital ties with foreign kings as a peace-pledge or mother of sons, or socially and psychologically as a cup-passing and peace-weaving queen within a hall. Wealhtheow becomes a peace-pledge to unite the Danes and Helmings; Hildeburh similarly unites the Danes and Frisians through her marriage; and Freawaru at least intends to pledge peace between the Danes and Heathobards. Such a role is predicated upon the woman's ability to bear children, to create blood ties, bonds to weave a "peace kinship."

In addition, woman functions domestically within the nation as a cup-passer during hall festivities of peace and joy after battle or contest. The mead-sharing ritual and the cup-passer herself come to symbolize peace-weaving and peace because they strengthen the societal and familial bonds between lord and retainers. First, the literal action of the peace-weaver as she passes the cup from warrior to warrior weaves an invisible web of peace: the order in which each man is served, according to his social position, reveals each man's dependence upon and responsibility toward another. For example, after Wealhtheow gives the cup to Hrothgar she bids him to be joyful at drinking as well as loving to his people. Then she offers it to the old retainers, then to the young retainers, and finally to the guest Beowulf. Second, her peace-weaving also takes a verbal form: her speeches accompanying the mead-sharing stress the peace and joy contingent upon the fulfillment of each man's duty to his nation. At the joyous celebration after Grendel's defeat Wealhtheow concludes her speeches with a tribute to the harmony of the present moment by reminding her tribe of its cause, that is, adherence to the *comitatus* ethic. Each man remains true to the other, each is loyal to the king, the nation is ready and alert, the drinking warriors attend to the ale-dispenser herself. . . .

Third, the peace-weaver herself emblematizes peace, for she appears in the poem with her mead-vessel only after a contest has been concluded. Thus Wealhtheow enters the hall only after the contest between Unferth and Beowulf; she does not appear again until after Beowulf has overcome Grendel, when the more elaborate feasting invites the peace-making speeches mentioned above.

Most of the other female characters figure as well in this middle section so that the female monster's adventures are framed by descriptions of other women for ironic contrast. . . .

PASSIVE ACCEPTANCE, NOT REVENGE

In the first part of the female monster's section, the idea is stressed that a kinswoman or mother must passively accept and not actively avenge the loss of her son. The story of the mother Hildeburh is recited by the scop [singer] early on the evening Grendel's mother will visit Heorot. The lay ends at line 1159; Grendel's mother enters the poem a mere hundred lines later when she attacks the Danish hall, as the Frisian contingent attacked the hall lodging Hildeburh's Danish brother in the *Finnsburh Fragment.* The *Beowulf* poet alters the focus of the fragment: he stresses the consequences of the surprise attack rather than the attack itself in order to reveal Hildeburh's maternal reactions to them.

Hildeburh is "unjustly" deprived of her Danish brother and Finnish son, but all she does, this "sad woman," is to mourn her loss with dirges and stoically place her son on the pyre. In fact, she can do nothing, caught in the very web she has woven as peace-pledge: her husband's men have killed her brother, her brother's men have killed her son. Later the Danish Hengest will avenge the feud with her husband Finn, whether she approves or not, by overwhelming the Frisians and returning Hildeburh to her original tribe. The point remains: the peace-pledge must accept a passive role precisely because the ties she knots bind *her*—she *is* the knot, the pledge of peace. Her fate interlaces with that of her husband and brothers through her role as a mother bearing a son: thus Hildeburh appropriately mourns the loss of her symbolic tie at the pyre, the failure of her self as peace-pledge, the loss of her identity. Like Hildeburh Grendel's dam will also lose her identity as mother, never having had an identity as peace-pledge to lose. . . .

Grendel's mother intent on avenging the loss of her son in the *present* attacks Heorot, her masculine aggression contrasting with the feminine passivity of both Hildeburh and Wealhtheow. Indeed, she resembles a grieving human mother: like Hildeburh she is guiltless and "gloomy-minded"; her journey to Heorot must be sorrowful for she "remembered her misery.". . .

Her attempts to avenge her son's death could be justified if she were human and male, for no *wergild* [compensation] has been offered to her by the homicide Beowulf. The role of the masculine avenger is emphasized throughout the passage in defining her motivation to attack: she performs the role of avenger "to avenge the death of her son." Whatever her maternal feelings, she actually fulfills the duty of the kinsman. Unlike Hildeburh, she cannot wait for a Hengest to resolve the feud in some way; unlike Freawaru, she cannot act as a peace-pledge to settle the feud. Tribeless, now kinless, forced to rely on her own might, she seizes and kills Æschere, Hrothgar's most beloved retainer, in an appropriate retribution for the loss of her own most beloved "retainer" and "lord"—her son. . . .

For a mother to "avenge" her son as if she were a retainer, he were her lord, and avenging more important than peace-making, is monstrous. . . .

This idea [that peace-weaving must ultimately fail] is implied in Hrothgar's sermon (1700–84), like the court celebration of Hygelac a part of the middle section belonging to Grendel's mother but apparently unrelated to it. In it Hrothgar describes three Christian vices in distinctly Germanic terms. Impelled by envy like Grendel, Heremod kills his "table-companions." Next the wealthy hall-ruler in his pride is attacked by the Adversary while his guardian conscience sleeps within the hall of his soul. So the monster that specifically epitomizes pride in *Beowulf,* as in Genesis, is female—Grendel's mother. . . .

Grendel's mother substitutes war-making for the peace-weaving of the queen out of a kind of selfish pride—if she were capable of recognizing it as such. Finally, this same hall ruler "covets angry-minded" the ornamented treasures God has previously given him by refusing to dispense any to his warriors. So the mock gold-king dragon avariciously [greedily] guards his treasure. Although the poet portrays the monsters as antitypes of Germanic ideals, his integument [covering] conceals a Christian idea. The city of man, whether located in a Germanic or Christian society, is always threatened by sin and failure.

Such sin alienates Christian man from self, neighbor, and God; it alienates Germanic man primarily from other men. Note that although in *Beowulf* each of the three monsters is described as guarding or possessing a hall, whether Heorot, a watery cavern, or a barrow, each remains isolated from humanity (and from each other—Grendel and his mother live together, but they never appear together in the poem until he is dead). Ideally when the retainer, the queen, and the gold-lord cooperate they constitute a viable nucleus of Germanic society: a retainer must have a gold-lord from whom to receive gold for his loyalty in battle; the peace-weaver must have a "loom"—the band of retainers and their lord, or two nations—upon which to weave peace.

Despite the poet's realization that these roles cannot be fulfilled in this world, this Germanic ideal provides structural and thematic unity for *Beowulf.* Grendel's mother does occupy a transitional position in the poem: as a "retainer" attacking Heorot she resembles Grendel, but as an "attacked ruler" of her own "hall" she resembles the dragon. As a monstrous mother and queen she perverts a role more important socially and symbolically than that of Grendel. . . .

The structural position of her episode in the poem, like woman's position as cup-passer among members of the nation, or as a peace-pledge between two nations, is similarly medial and transitional, but successfully so.

The Finn Episode and Revenge in *Beowulf*

Martin Camargo

As the longest digression in *Beowulf,* the relevance of
the Finn episode puzzles many readers. Scholar
Martin Camargo of the University of Alabama argues
that the story in this digression serves to cast doubt
on the revenge ethic, ironically undercutting
Beowulf's heroism. Camargo contends that the
revenge ethic is further undercut by the suffering
and injustice experienced by the women of the
poem, whose peaceful values represent the poem's
only alternative to vengeance.

The Finn episode in *Beowulf* (lines 1068–1159) has continued to attract a disproportionate amount of scholarly attention for the better part of a century. The allusive manner of
its telling has long taxed the abilities of philologists to determine the precise sense of the lines, while its position within
the narrative has challenged the ingenuity of a growing
number of critics who have sought to establish (or to question) its relevance. . . .

The following, uncontroversial outline of the story suf-
fices for the present purposes: The Danish chieftain Hnaef
and his band of retainers are attacked at night by their host
the Frisian king Finn, husband of Hnaef's sister Hildeburh.
After several days of fighting, in which Hnaef and, on the
other side, Hildeburh's son are among those killed, neither
side can achieve a decisive victory. Hengest, the new leader
of the Danes, reluctantly makes peace with Finn, and the
Danish and Frisian dead are burned side by side. The
uneasy truce is broken at winter's end when the Danes turn
upon and kill Finn, plunder his treasure, and carry
Hildeburh back to her people.

Confronted by this "digression" for the first time, most

From "The Finn Episode and the Tragedy of Revenge in *Beowulf,*" by Martin Camargo,
Studies in Philology, vol. 78. Copyright © 1981 by the University of North Carolina
Press. Used by permission of the publisher and the author.

readers are uncertain about its relevance to the matter at hand. Why, one asks, does the poet interrupt his narrative at the height of the festivities honoring Beowulf's victory over Grendel to spend more than ninety lines telling the story of a bloody feud between a band of Danes and the Frisian king Finn? . . .

A STORY OF TREACHERY AND REVENGE

The festival occasioned by the deliverance from Grendel is plainly the high point of joy in the poem. Never again will we see such unrestrained rejoicing. A burden of twelve years' duration has just been lifted from the shoulders of the Danes, and they are celebrating as if there were no tomorrow. The poet clearly wished to emphasize the extremity of their rejoicing, for he spends, omitting the three digressions (a total of 130 lines), over 250 lines describing the victory party. So happy are the Danes, in fact, that they manage to forget that Grendel has a mother lurking on the moors, and "his avenger still lived / after that battle" (1256–57).[1] Their happiness, if illusory, is complete. Thus, the abrupt introduction of a story of treachery, bloody revenge, and innocent suffering has the effect of a powerful contrast, coming at the very peak of the festivities. For if the events glorify the Danes, the tone of the episode is certainly tragic. The allusion, at this point, to past battles which brought swift and fatal recrimination, brings out vividly the transience of the Scyldings' joy. The chain of revenge is unbroken, and sorrow will be renewed in Heorot on the morrow; a sorrow all the more bitter because least expected and following so closely upon heartfelt joy. . . .

Earlier critics have not only overlooked this powerful contrast between joyous feast and grisly feud, but have also frequently gone on to misidentify the source of the episode's pathos. They have consistently attributed this pathos to the episode's "tragic" qualities, but have had some difficulty agreeing about who is the tragic figure and why. Early scholarship tended to focus on Hengest's dilemma almost to the point of excluding Hildeburh, and though Hildeburh has been assigned a more conspicuous position in most recent scholarship, she has yet to receive the attention she deserves.

1. In this essay, all translations of Old English are taken from Howell D. Chickering Jr., *Beowulf: A Dual Language Edition.* New York: Anchor Books, 1977.

Hengest and, to a lesser extent, Finn may be the chief *actors* in the tragedy enacted at Finnsburg, but we are made to view their actions in terms of their effects on the tragic victim Hildeburh. When the scop announces, in good epic fashion, the subject of his song, he speaks not of the wrath of Hengest but rather the sorrows of Hildeburh:

> No need at all   that Hildeburh praise
> the faith of the "giants";   guiltless herself,
> she lost her loved ones   in that clash of shields,
> her son and brother   —they were born to fall,
> slain by spear-thrusts.   She knew deep grief.
> Not without cause   did Hoc's daughter mourn
> the web's short measure   that fated morning
> when she saw their bodies,   her murdered kinsmen,
> under the skies   where she had known
> her greatest joy. (1071–80a)

Nor does he conclude with praise of the Danes' valor, as might be expected had his story sprung from purely patriotic motives. Instead we are left with the image of the destitute Hildeburh, carried away from Finnsburg precisely like a piece of the booty. . . .

Helpless to avert the disaster, she must first endure the loss of a son and a brother, and then, when the truce is finally broken, see her husband cut down "with his troop" before her very eyes. Blameless herself, she has lost all that had mattered to her in life. . . .

THE SUFFERING OF THE FEMALE CHARACTERS

Hildeburh's fate, moreover, is shared by nearly all of the female characters in *Beowulf*. The connection between her tragedy and the similar one forecast for Wealhtheow is the most obvious. Before the image of Hildeburh has had a chance to fade, the poet brings forth Hrothgar's queen, ominously alluding to the unhappy bond which joins the two women:

> Wealhtheow came forth,
> glistening in the gold   to great the good pair,
> uncle and nephew;   their peace was still firm,
> each true to the other. (1162b–5a)

The disaster at Finnsburg casts its pall over Wealhtheow's ministrations, creating an ironic distance between her hopes for the future and the bloodshed that every member of the audience knows will follow. The same theme is again expressed, though less dramatically, in Beowulf's later prophesy concerning Freawaru and Ingeld (2020–69). His speech is a perfect account of the revenge ethic in action, which, by stressing the helplessness of the woman, cannot but recall the Finn episode. No less significant is the fact that at the end of the poem a woman is again singled out to represent the sorrow of the Geats at Beowulf's funeral pyre and to voice their fears of future strife.

Far from acquiescing in the inevitability of the suffering of these representative women, the poet takes special pains to demonstrate its injustice. He makes us feel the deepest outrage at the constant warring among men by stressing the innocence of its chief victims, the women. The women, in fact, are practically defined as peace-bringers. Wealhtheow, in particular, is the embodiment of concord. In her various appearances (611–41, 1162–1233, 2016–19) she actively creates harmony by carrying the mead cup from man to man. Yet this exemplary woman, we are constantly reminded, will get bitter sorrow for her reward. . . .

THE DARK SIDE OF HEROIC VIRTUE

In Hildeburh, Hrethel, and the unnamed father who must see his son hanged without hope for recompense (2444–62), the inadequacy of the revenge ethic is displayed in a way that must arouse pity and fear. Each passage treats the theme of vengeance tainted with strife among kin from the point of view of innocent victims, and each passage occurs at an emotional highpoint in the action. The setting of Hrethel's story shares an especially important feature with that of Finn's. Both stories immediately precede the taking of revenge by the hero Beowulf. In each case Beowulf is about to perform to the utmost the role of Germanic hero and, in the second case, protector of his people. Just as he descended into the pool alone to face Grendel's mother, so too does he enter the barrow alone to face the dragon. Yet at the very points in the narrative where the hero displays most gloriously his heroic virtue by risking his life to avenge a feud singlehandedly, the poet deliberately chose to insert two of the most disturbing passages in the poem; passages, moreover, which seem designed to question, by portraying its darker side, the very heroic virtue the hero is about to put into action.

The juxtaposition of heroic virtue, on the one hand, and innocent suffering and kin-killing on the other seems incon-

FEUDS AND JUSTICE IN *BEOWULF*

Many critics of Beowulf *have argued that the revenge ethic of the poem leads to an interminable cycle of violence. From his anthropological perspective, John M. Hill counters this view, suggesting that the poem clearly endorses the "good of violence" in some situations.*

Some anthropologists think that blood feuds are in effect interminable, even if a given feud series is compromised through compensation. The blood debt is never quite even, as no two groups are perfectly balanced in prestige and power, and the psychology of debt looks for repayment with interest. Others consider that any feud is in principle resolvable, given the shifting compositions of the groups involved over time.

This dispute seems to founder over priorities. Is feud some definable state that in turn defines groups? Or do competing groups fall into a feuding relationship that is susceptible to changes in the constitution of the groups and the climate of competition? I incline to the latter view although *Beowulf* does not say much about this directly. Indirectly, in its underwriting of just revenge through divinity, king, and hero, *Beowulf* clearly countenances the good of violence in situations where one seeks a justifiable settlement rather than dark pleasures. And directly, in the alliance Beowulf announces between Geats and Danes, the poem shows that groups who once exchanged hostilities—whether called feuds or not—can put that behind in an arrangement of mutual support.

gruous only to one determined to find in the glorification of the former the purpose of the poem. To a less partial observer, they are but two sides of the same coin, while to a Christian they are the same side viewed in different lights. For as every Christian knows, and as the poet keeps reminding us, the origin of all strife was Cain's vengeful murder of his brother Abel. From the poet's Christian perspective, all strife involves kinsmen because all men are brothers. Any code which has for its central tenet the duty of revenge is therefore, from that same perspective, fundamentally defective.

Not the least of the qualities which raise Beowulf above his fellows and mark him as the ideal pagan hero are his abhorrence of kin-killing and his exemplary devotion to his own kinsmen, especially Hygelac. . . . Yet in spite of his high sense of loyalty—a sense of loyalty all too rare among the other personages who figure in the poem, he still falls far short of the Christian ideal. With all of his virtues, he still lives according to the Old Law of retribution. He recognizes the inefficacy of human efforts to establish peace, but knows no alternative to the rule of an eye for an eye.

Nowhere is the limitation of his knowledge so evident as at the point where he enthusiastically embraces the heroic ethic: "Better it is for every man / to avenge his friend than mourn overmuch" (1384–5). Having just witnessed the effects of this attitude at Finnsburg, the audience would have greeted Beowulf's sentiments with less wholehearted approbation than might otherwise have been the case. . . . As he speaks the chastened listener can hardly help thinking of situations, like that at Finnsburg, in which swift and violent revenge, whatever the motivation, is not so manifestly a just and proper course of action. Equally evident is the fact that Beowulf, placed in such a situation, would respond in all ways just as Hengest did, except that his vengeance would be swifter in coming and, because of his unique prowess, more "personally" administered. . . .

THE VICIOUS CYCLE OF REVENGE

The real source of the tragedy in the Finn episode as in the entire poem is the whole cycle of revenge leading to further revenge. Steeped in an ethic which demands an eye for an eye, Hengest has in reality no choice. He is given ample opportunity to forgive—the terms of the treaty are more favorable than he could reasonably expect; but we know and the poet's audience knew that he would not. Ignorant of Christian compassion, he cannot break out of the vicious circle of retaliation, just as the Heathobards cannot forgive the Danes nor the Swedes the Geats. No matter how noble it is to avenge one's lord or one's kin, it is ultimately hopeless: another avenger will always appear and more innocent people will suffer needlessly. The only effective remedy to the fatalism bred by this realization is to break the chain which began when Cain murdered his brother Abel and embrace an ethic in which compassion, perhaps even forgiveness, finds a place alongside the more warlike virtues.

The function of the Finn episode, in short, is to cast doubt on the revenge ethic at the very point in the narrative where such a code appears most glorious. The poet first tempts us with the exhilaration of Beowulf's spectacular and seemingly

just resolution of the feud with Grendel, and then forcefully
reminds us that in the normal affairs of men revenge is seldom such a clear-cut matter. Usually there is no way of
telling who is right and who is wrong, and everybody loses,
as Grendel's mother reminds the revellers and as the poet
reminds us:

> No good exchange,
> that those on both sides   had to pay with the lives
> of kinsmen and friends. (1304b–6a)

The poet does not again make such effective use of historical allusion to heighten dramatic tension until the final
scenes of the poem, when Geatish history is interwoven with
the dragon-fight and Beowulf's death against a background
of impending disaster. Nor does the poet's attitude toward
vengeance ever come across more clearly than in the doom-
fraught lines of the poem's second part. But the hero's death
and the prophesies of disaster for his people would not be
nearly so disturbing had we not been shown the darker side
of glory, the murky depths hidden by the dazzling surface,
even as we admired Beowulf in his prime. At a moment of
high excitement in the narration of his poem, the poet intro-
duces a tale of cruel revenge, the pathetic tone of which is in
startling contrast with the joyous surroundings. The pressure of the dramatic situation and the complex of parallels
to feuds past, present, and to come has the effect of tele-
scoping all history into one portentous moment. The temporary, illusory joy of the banquet is in stark contrast to the
ever-present reality of inevitable bloodshed and renewal of
hostilities. In the world of *Beowulf,* Cain's sin is constantly
reenacted; any peace purchased by violence is precarious
and certain to be overturned before long, with tragic consequences for the innocent and guilty alike. Neither the
strength and wisdom of a Beowulf or a Hrothgar, nor the
"peace-weaving" of a Hildeburh or a Wealhtheow suffice to
insure peace and prosperity. Such tranquility is always
short-lived—powerful kings die without heir, conjugal
affection cools in the heat of other passions, and kinsman
rises against kinsman. As long as he considers worldly riches and honor, won by force of arms, the supreme good, even
Beowulf is powerless to prevent further genocide.

The only hope for sure peace, the poet clearly implies, lies
in the love and compassion which Christianity offers as its
ideal and which the women in *Beowulf* seem to symbolize.

That the poet nowhere points this moral explicitly is a tribute to his poetic talents. By neither depreciating Beowulf's genuine virtues nor constructing an elaborate allegorical subtext, he is able to make his Christian audience experience directly and powerfully the most important tenet of the faith they all shared. Had Beowulf been less admirable, or had his death not brought with it such dire consequences for so many real people, the members of the audience could have indulged more safely in their vicarious return to the excitement of the heroic past. By linking that past to Old Testament history, by making clear that the hero is the best of men acting in strict accordance with the best rules of conduct then available to him, and finally by showing how far even this exemplary pagan's beliefs fall short of the Christian ideal, the poet instead forces his audience to recognize, and thence to abhor the lingering vestiges of paganism in their own hearts. Lacking the universal love which is the essence of Christianity, Beowulf is as far removed from the true Christian as Grendel is from Beowulf. By skillfully revealing the traces of Grendel in Beowulf, the poet held up to his audience a mirror in which they might view the traces of Beowulf in themselves.

Treachery and Betrayal in *Beowulf*

Hugh Magennis

In this excerpt from his book *Images of Community in Old English Poetry,* Hugh Magennis, professor of English at Queen's University of Belfast, argues that the depiction of Anglo-Saxon society in *Beowulf* was not intended to be glowing and nostalgic. On the contrary, this is a society riddled with internal treachery, a society in which betrayal is the "rule rather than the exception." From this perspective, the integrity and lack of treachery in Beowulf himself are all the more remarkable.

The nobility of the hero and of other leading figures in *Beowulf* is glowingly celebrated in the poem, earning the approval both of the narrator and of other choric [commenting] voices. Beowulf's unflinching resoluteness, his wisdom and his loyalty, first to his lord and then to his followers, identify him as a model of heroic conduct. The closing lines of the poem, mentioning his quality of generosity as well as eagerness for praise, testify to the esteem in which this hero is held in his world. Like Bede's Edwin, he shuns all that is meanminded. A passage in praise of Beowulf after his triumphant return from Denmark to Geatland, emphasizes his lack of savagery–'his mind was not savage'—and comments especially on his honourable conduct towards his own companions. Never did he slay them when they had been drinking: 'Not at all did he slay his hearth-companions when they were drunk.' A few lines earlier the poet had contrasted Beowulf with those who plot the death of a comrade: 'So must a kinsman act, not at all weave a net of malice for another by secret cunning, prepare the death of a close companion' (2166–80).

Such views of the greatness of Beowulf are amply justified by his actions in the poem. There is, however, a certain dis-

Reprinted by permission of the publisher from *Images of Community in Old English Poetry,* by Hugh Magennis. Copyright © 1996 by Cambridge University Press.

quieting aspect to some of this praise. That Beowulf was not savage-minded and never turned violently on his compan- ions or plotted the death of a kinsman hardly seems much of a point in his favour for the poet to choose to highlight. What sort of warrior would do such things anyway? In a context in which honourable behaviour rather than treachery was expected, these instances of Beowulf's nobility would sound like faint praise, anticlimactic and unremarkable.

A CLIMATE OF TREACHERY

But this suggestion of a climate of treachery is precisely what is borne out by an examination of the world of *Beowulf* as a whole. The poem presents great acts of virtue, but in a context of predominant weakness and failure, epitomized particularly by failures of loyalty and trust. In *Beowulf* it may be Grendel who is described as 'encompassed with treach- ery', but it is the human characters, rather than the mon- sters, who are shown as acting with deceit and treachery. The pervasive presence of treachery and deceit contributes decisively to the the sense of pessimism which characterizes the poem's presentation of pre-Christian Germanic society. *Beowulf* centres on noble characters and praiseworthy actions, but throughout the poem these characters and actions are encompassed and constricted by the kinds of *inwitnet* 'nets of malice', alluded to in the above quotation.

Most people in *Beowulf* are not like Beowulf and the handful of other admirable characters. Treachery between tribes is perhaps implied already in the reference, in the first fitt [section], to the eventual destruction of Heorot, the result of the enmity of father-in-law and son-in-law in the sup- pressed feud between the Danes and Heathobards. Beowulf himself foresees oaths being broken between the two sides and he expresses his doubts about the trustworthiness of the Heathobards. The idea of treachery *within* tribes is striking- ly evident among the Danes and is shown as afflicting them in the past and future, as well as being symbolically tolerat- ed in the poem's present in the person of the brother-killer Unferth. Unferth has been seen by some critics as a figure of disorder at Heorot, but his great crime is that of treachery. Disturbingly, however, Unferth's treachery appears to be accepted by society. This brother-killer has an honoured place in the hall, sitting at the feet of Hrothgar, and his crime, though no secret, is mentioned only by Beowulf, as a result of taunting provocation from Unferth himself: 'You became the killer of your brothers, your closest kinsmen; for that you must suffer damnation in hell, though your cleverness avails you' (587–89).

The enormity of Unferth's crime is fully acknowledged in the eternal punishment to which Beowulf here appeals, but it is ignored among the Danes. Indeed, Beowulf himself appears disconcertingly well-disposed towards Unferth outside the one scene of their altercation. With regard to Unferth, as to others in the poem, Beowulf accepts the fact of treachery in society with considerable equanimity, as though, despite his own high standards, he does not have high expectations for the conduct of others. Beowulf's essential concern throughout is with his own conduct rather than with the imperfection of other people. It is because of the faithlessness of his own men that he will face the dragon alone at the end of the poem. Wiglaf rebukes the other warriors, but Beowulf himself does not dwell on their disloyalty, being preoccupied instead by how he himself has acted.

Treachery among the Danes in the past is evident in the reference to the murderous savagery of Heremod, a former king. Heremod, unlike Beowulf, *did* turn on his close companions—'in his anger he destroyed his table-companions.' Heremod forfeited the loyalty of his people and was 'betrayed into the power of his enemies.' . . .

TREACHERY IN THE FUTURE

Treachery among the Danes in the future is also emphasized in the poem, undercutting the scenes of revelry in celebration of the defeats of Grendel and Grendel's mother. The narrator refers to the *facenstafas* 'treacherous arts', which Hrothulf will practise in future days, and comments that at the time of the foreground events of the poem there is 'as yet' trust between Hrothgar and Hrothulf. The sentence immediately following this observation refers pointedly to the presence of Unferth in the company of the Scyldings and to the trust that they have in his spirit. Wealhtheow perceives only loyalty among the Danes and looks forward in sanguine fashion to Hrothulf's protection of her own children if he should outlive Hrothgar: 'I know that my Hrothulf is gracious, that he will treat these youths with honour, if you, lord of the Scyldings, should leave the world before him; I expect that he will repay our sons with generosity, if he remembers all the favours that the two of us have formerly done for him for his pleasure and honour, while he was a child' (1180–78). The poem makes it clear that such optimism will not be borne out by events.

The faithlessness of Beowulf's own warriors in the closing part of the poem is not dwelt on by the hero himself, but the seriousness of their transgression of the code of loyalty is fully apparent, and is particularly castigated by Wiglaf, the faithful follower. At the end of the poem a bleak time to come is forecast for the Geats, who have failed their lord in his fight—on their behalf—against the dragon. For the Geats to have deserted Beowulf at his time of need may be regarded as the equivalent to their having fled from an army led by the king, which we have seen to be a grave crime in late Anglo-Saxon law. There is no need, however, to appeal to particular laws to appreciate the fault of the Geats, since the Germanic revulsion against disloyalty to a lord, recorded as early as Tacitus, is keenly felt by the warriors themselves. They themselves are *scamiende*, 'ashamed', as they endure the rebuke of Wiglaf, who reminds them that 'for any warrior death is better than a life of disgrace.' . . . The poet refers to the faint-hearted Geatish warriors explicitly as *treowlogan*, 'troth-breakers'.

OUTCAST LIKE CAIN

The future that Wiglaf predicts for the Geats is one of alienation and desolation, in which they will wander about without right to land: 'Each man of the tribe must wander, destitute of his land-right.'

The image has overtones of the punishment of the betrayer Cain, who is directly referred to several times in the poem: Grendel is associated with the dwelling-places of the kindred of Cain; Cain had been banished by the Lord far from humankind after his crime of brother-killing; as a result of his crime, he was outlawed, marked with murder and had to settle in the wilderness; the race of giants descended from him had been destroyed in the Flood; the poem also says that Grendel was descended from Cain. The legend of Cain is thus familiarly alluded to in *Beowulf*, but the idea of the Cain figure is also insistently drawn upon outside such references, in the poem's treatment of acts of treachery and betrayal. It is there in the words of Wiglaf just quoted, and in the account of Heremod, who after he destroyed his table-companions turned away alone from the joys of men: 'until he turned away alone, the famous chieftain, from the joys of men.'

Hæthcyn's tragic killing of his brother Herebald, though apparently an accident, bears a Cain-like weight of unatonable guilt. It is described as a crime, 'sinfully committed, wearying to the heart.'

Unferth, the poem's other brother-killer, may have escaped the fate of Cain in the present life, but Beowulf is confident that this Cain figure will receive his punishment in the next. For other betrayers, as Wiglaf perceives with regard to the disgraced Geats, their sin brings its own punishment in this world, a punishment whose physical hardship may be seen as, like that of Cain, reflecting a spiritual alienation and annihilation.

The message of *Beowulf* concerning treachery and betrayal is that they are evils destructive to society and to self. And yet the reality of the poem's world is that treachery and betrayal are the rule rather than the exception. In Bede's *Historia Ecclesiastica* treachery is associated with external enemies; in *Beowulf* it is within. Unferth retains his place at the heart of society. The frequency of acts of deceit and betrayal in *Beowulf* militates against the view of the poem as a nostalgic evocation of a glamorous Germanic past. The poem shows admiration for the noble aspirations of the pre-Christian Germanic world, but sets these aspirations beside a perceived reality of predominant weakness and failure. *Beowulf* shows acute awareness of the discrepancy between ideal and reality in an imperfect world, and it encourages its audience to consider the significance of this discrepancy. At the end of the poem the audience is led to identify not with the superhuman Beowulf but with the mourning Geats who honour him and contemplate a future without him.

The Digressions in *Beowulf*

David Wright

The digressions in *Beowulf* are especially puzzling to first-time readers trying to follow the main plot and themes. British scholar David Wright points out in the following essay that the many digressions and episodes are not accidental, but rather serve as indirect commentary and context for the main plot. The distressing and violent feuds described in the digressions serve, in Wright's view, to cast a pall over Beowulf's achievements.

[Turning] to the structure of *Beowulf:* one of its characteristics is the extraordinary number of episodes and digressions that are contained in it. Many of these considerably puzzled the early students of the poem, who invented a number of ingenious but unsatisfactory theories to account for them, theories which usually postulated either a composite authorship for the work or the existence of one or more interpolators. It is now generally agreed—and indeed obvious—that *Beowulf* is the work of a single poet, and that this poet was a Christian. In a brilliant essay, *The Digressions in Beowulf,* M. Adrien Bonjour has discussed the artistic relevance of these episodes and asides. He concluded that the poet of *Beowulf* knew what he was about: everything that he put into his poem is there to add something to the effect of the whole. Far from being a rambling, incoherent affair, the poem is built up of themes, motifs, contrasts, and parallels, and is in fact as sophisticated in its construction and use of allusion as *The Waste Land* of T.S. Eliot. One example is the funeral of Scyld Scefing, with which the poem opens, foreshadowing Beowulf's obsequies [funeral rites] at the end. Another may be found when Beowulf's defeat of Grendel is celebrated by one of Hrothgar's men in a song of praise, and the singer compares the hero with the mythical

From pages 13, 14–16 of the Introduction by David Wright to *Beowulf,* translated by David Wright (Penguin Classics, 1957). Copyright © David Wright, 1957. Reprinted by permission of Penguin UK.

Sigemund who won fame by killing a dragon: thus bringing to Beowulf's first exploit an echo of his last. And so on.

HISTORICAL REFERENCES

But to a modern audience some of the episodes and allusions are obscure because they depend for their understanding on a knowledge of the history of Scandinavian dynasties, a knowledge which the poet of *Beowulf* was able to assume on the part of the audience he was addressing. For instance, the eventual burning of Hrothgar's hall, and the usurpation of the Danish throne by his nephew Hrothulf, are more than once alluded to in the poem, though these events lie outside the actual scope of its story. The implications of such references were not lost on the Anglo-Saxon audience. They did not miss the ironic and sinister overtones of the incident at the banquet celebrating the defeat of Grendel, when Wealhtheow, Hrothgar's wife, commends her sons to the generosity of her husband's nephew Hrothulf. For this was the man who, as we know from other sources, was destined to wade in her children's blood to the Danish throne. And earlier, at the same banquet, Hrothgar's court poet sings a song about Finn, which at first appears to have nothing to do with the main theme of the poem. Yet it affords another of the grim and ironically-hinted analogues of which the *Beowulf* poet was so fond. For an old blood-feud was at that moment smouldering between Hrothgar's people and another tribe, the Heathobards; and, as we learn later on in the poem itself, at the time of the banquet Hrothgar was engaged in trying to settle this feud by marrying his own daughter Freawaru to Ingeld, the leader of the Heathobards. And what is the song of Finn about? It tells of a blood-feud, in which a queen is torn between opposing loyalties owed to her husband and to her brother, who fought on different sides; of the official settling of this feud, which was yet so ineradicable that it burst out again, disastrously. Thus the song of Finn from one point of view suggests a left-handed prefiguring of the luckless result of Hrothgar's attempt to settle the Danish-Heathobard feud, and of the dilemma in which his own daughter Freawaru, divided in loyalty between her husband and her father, was to find herself.

AN ATMOSPHERE OF DOOM

In this way the *Beowulf* poet builds up an atmosphere of doom, which Beowulf's victories over Grendel and Grendel's mother scarcely dispel. It is a human evil—the Heathobard feud—and not the monsters, which in the end destroy Hrothgar's palace. This effect is paralleled in the second part of the poem, which deals with the Dragon fight, in the reminders of the quarrels of Beowulf's own people, the Geats, with the Franks and Swedes, and in the indications that after the death of Beowulf there will be little to prevent the enemies of the Geats from annihilating them. In a sense Grendel and his mother are a manifestation of the evil that will overtake the Danes, and the Dragon of the disaster which is to destroy the Geats. Many minor touches go to the creation of this aura of overhanging catastrophe. To take one instance, the poet interrupts his description of Beowulf's fight with the Dragon to give a long and apparently irrelevant account of the history of the sword with which his kinsman Wiglaf comes to the hero's rescue. But the point about the sword is that it was a trophy taken in battle from the brother of the Swedish king by Wiglaf's father: and it is thus a reminder of an unsettled blood-feud, and can therefore furnish the Swedes with an excuse to declare war when Wiglaf inherits the Geat throne after Beowulf's death.

Another effect of what are called 'the historical elements' in *Beowulf*—the subsidiary stories of the Danes and the Geats—is to give the poem greater depth and verisimilitude. Hrothgar, the Danish king, is a 'historical' character, and the site of his palace of Heorot has been identified with the village of Leire on the island of Seeland in Denmark. The Geat king Hygelac really existed, and his unlucky expedition against the Franks, referred to several times in the poem, is mentioned by Gregory of Tours in the *Historia Francorum* and has been given the approximate date of A.D. 521. We must remember that to Anglo-Saxons of the eighth century the main events of the wars and feuds of the Danes, Swedes, and Geats of the sixth century were probably quite as familiar as those of the Napoleonic wars are to a modern reader. Beowulf, Grendel, and the Dragon clearly belong to the 'mythical elements'—though it is worth noting that these distinctions might have appeared unimportant to the audience of *Beowulf.*

AN IRONIC EFFECT

But the main relevance of the subsidiary stories of the feuds between the Danes and the Heathobards, and between the Geats and the Swedes and the Franks, to the whole poem, lies in the ironic effect which the poet extracts from them so often and unfailingly. After describing how Hrothgar built Heorot, 'the greatest banqueting hall ever known', and picturing its magnificence and the feast held to celebrate its completion, the poet immediately reminds us: 'Yet it was to endure leaping flames, when in the course of time a deadly feud between Hrothgar and his son-in-law should be kindled by an act of vengeance.' It is at this significant point that Grendel is introduced: the outcast monster who, angered by the song of Creation which is sung in Heorot, begins to ravage the hall. And generally it may be said that the poet uses the subsidiary 'historical' stories to hammer home the temporal nature of Beowulf's heroic achievements. There is irony latent in the fact that although Beowulf purges Heorot and kills the Dragon, the Danes and the Geats whom he tries to help are destined to be destroyed by the consequences of their own deeds.

Chronology

A.D. 400–600

The Age of Germanic Migration; Britain is invaded and settled by tribes from Scandinavia and northern Europe, primarily the Angles, the Saxons, and the Jutes.

410

Rome is sacked by Germanic invaders, beginning the dissolution of the Roman Empire; Rome formally renounces control of Britain.

CA. 516

Battle of Mount Badon in south-central England; the army of the Celtic leader Ambrosius Aurelianus (the legendary King Arthur?) defeats an army of the invading Saxons; recorded in Gildas (A.D. 540).

521

The death of King Hygelac during a raid on the lower Rhine River is recorded in Frankish historical annals. According to our poem, Beowulf took part in this raid and was a survivor of the battle.

597

St. Augustine arrives in region of Kent, beginning the conversion of England to Christianity.

CA. 615

By this date, the Angles and the Saxons have effectively ended all resistance by the Celts, the original inhabitants of Britain.

CA. 625

The ship burial in a mound at Sutton Hoo, Suffolk, England (discovered in 1939).

660–700

Caedmon the poet flourishes; according to the historian Bede, Caedmon was the first great Christian poet in England.

CA. 700

The Lindisfarne Gospels written and decorated at the Lindesfarne monastery in northern England.

700–850

Beowulf composed during this period.

731

Bede completes his *Ecclesiastical History*, a history of England and the Christian Church in England up to 731.

781

English scholar Alcuin meets Charlemagne and soon leaves York (northern England) for the king's court.

793–795

Early Danish Viking raids on monasteries at Lindesfarne and Iona.

866–900

The First Viking Wars.

869

Vikings defeat and kill Edmund, king of East Anglia.

878

Alfred the Great defeats Viking army at Battle of Edington; the Vikings settle in East Anglia.

991

Battle of Maldon; the Vikings defeat an English army led by Byrhtnoth.

CA. 1000

The one extant copy of *Beowulf* (now in the British Museum) is transcribed.

1013

The English are defeated by the Vikings; Swein, king of Denmark, begins rule of England.

1042

Rule of England returns to the West Saxon king Edward the Confessor.

1066

Battle of Hastings; English army defeated by the French Norman army of William the Conqueror.

CA. 1390

Chaucer writes *The Canterbury Tales*.

FOR FURTHER RESEARCH

EDITIONS AND TRANSLATIONS OF *BEOWULF*

Editor's Note: All editions cited here have useful introductions and/or commentary.

Michael Alexander, Beowulf: *A Verse Translation.* Harmondsworth, England: Penguin Books, 1973.

William Alfred, *Beowulf,* in *Medieval Epics.* New York: Modern Library, 1963.

Howell D. Chickering Jr., Beowulf: *A Dual-Language Edition.* 2nd ed. Garden City, NY: Anchor-Doubleday, 1982. This edition contains an extensive and accessible running commentary on the poem. Very useful to first-time readers.

Kevin Crossley-Holland, *Beowulf.* Introduction by Bruce Mitchell. London: Farrar, Straus, & Giroux, 1968.

Stanley B. Greenfield, *A Readable* Beowulf: *The Old English Epic Newly Translated.* Introduction by Alain Renoir. Carbondale: Southern Illinois University Press, 1982.

Constance B. Hieatt, Beowulf *and Other Old English Poems.* Introduction by A. Kent Hieatt. New York: Bantam, 1982.

Marc Hudson, Beowulf: *A Translation and Commentary.* Lewisburg, PA: Bucknell University Press, 1990.

Marijane Osborn, Beowulf: *A Verse Translation with Treasure of the Ancient North.* Berkeley and Los Angeles: University of California Press, 1984.

Burton Raffel, *Beowulf.* 1963. Reprint, Amherst: University of Massachusetts Press, 1971.

Frederick R. Rebsamen, Beowulf: *A Verse Translation.* New York: HarperCollins, 1991.

Michael Swanton, Beowulf: *Edited with an Introduction. Notes, and New Prose Translation.* Manchester: Manchester University Press, 1978.

Barry Tharaud, *Beowulf.* Illustrations by Rockwell Kent. Niwot: University Press of Colorado, 1990.

Joseph F. Tuso, ed., Beowulf: *The Donaldson Translation,*

Backgrounds and Sources, Criticism. New York: W.W. Norton, 1975.

CRITICAL STUDIES OF *BEOWULF*

Peter S. Baker, ed., Beowulf: *Basic Readings.* New York: Garland, 1995. A collection of "classic" scholarly essays; most are aimed at advanced readers of the poem.

Robert E. Bjork and John D. Niles, eds., *A* Beowulf *Handbook.* Lincoln: University of Nebraska Press, 1997. Though most of the material in this handbook is aimed at advanced readers of *Beowulf,* it is currently the most comprehensive, up-to-date guide to the poem. The introduction, *"Beowulf,* Truth, and Meaning," by John Niles, is particularly recommended.

Harold Bloom, ed., *Modern Critical Interpretations of* Beowulf. New York: Chelsea House, 1987.

R.W. Chambers, *"Beowulf": An Introduction to the Study of the Poem.* 3rd ed. With a supplement by C.L. Wrenn. Cambridge: Cambridge University Press, 1959.

George Clark, *Beowulf.* Boston: Twayne, 1990. A very readable and useful overview of the poem and its interpretations.

Donald K. Fry, ed., *The "Beowulf" Poet: A Collection of Essays.* Englewood Cliffs, NJ: Prentice-Hall, 1968.

R.D. Fulk, ed., *Interpretations of* Beowulf: *A Critical Anthology.* Bloomington: Indiana University Press, 1991. A useful collection, though most essays are at the graduate student level.

Margaret E. Goldsmith, *The Mode and Meaning of* Beowulf. London: Athlone, 1970.

Stanley B. Greenfield, *"Beowulf* and Epic Tragedy," *Comparative Literature* 14 (1962): 91–105.

John M. Hill, *The Cultural World in* Beowulf. Toronto: University of Toronto Press, 1995.

Bernard F. Huppé, *The Hero in the Earthly City: A Reading of* Beowulf. MRTS 33. Binghamton: State University of New York Press, 1984.

Edward B. Irving Jr., *A Reading of* Beowulf. New Haven, CT: Yale University Press, 1968.

——, *Rereading* Beowulf. Philadelphia: University of Pennsylvania Press, 1989.

Lewis E. Nicholson, *An Anthology of "Beowulf" Criticism.* South Bend, IN: University of Notre Dame Press, 1963. These useful essays all support Christian interpretations of the poem.

John D. Niles, *Beowulf: The Poem and Its Tradition.* Cambridge, MA: Harvard University Press, 1983.

J.D.A. Ogilvy and Donald C. Baker, *Reading* Beowulf: *An Introduction to the Poem, Its Background, and Its Style.* Norman: University of Oklahoma Press, 1983. Contains much introductory-level, accessible background on the poem.

Marijane Osborn, "The Great Feud: Scriptural History and Strife in *Beowulf*," *PMLA* 93 (1978): 973–81.

Fred C. Robinson, "History, Religion, and Culture," in *Approaches to Teaching* Beowulf. Ed. Jess B. Bessinger Jr. and Robert F. Yeager. New York: Modern Language Association, 1984.

Thomas A. Shippey, *Beowulf.* London: Edward Arnold, 1978.

Kenneth Sisam, *The Structure of* Beowulf. Oxford: Clarendon Press, 1965.

Dorothy Whitelock, *The Audience of* Beowulf. Rev. ed. Oxford: Clarendon Press, 1958.

INDEX

Allegory of Love, The (Lewis), 50

Anglo-Saxon culture, 17, 19, 20, 61
  as basis for modern society, 47
  and conflict with modern values, 49, 52
  ideals of, 32, 33
    and duty to kinsmen, 40-41
    and fusion with Christianity, 36-37
    organized around leader, 17, 104-105
    violence/warfare of, 19, 35
  see also Beowulf, author of; *Beowulf,* historical background of; themes; women

Audience of Beowulf, The (Whitelock), 42

Augustine, Saint, 83

Bacon, Francis, 51
Baker, Donald C., 17, 69
barrow. *See* Beowulf, burial of
Bede, Saint, 104, 120, 124
  on fifth-century migrations, 38
  on virtue of kings, 43, 44
Benson, Larry D., 89
Beowulf, 14
  as antiquarian when written, 30
  audience of, 90, 126
  author of, 14, 15, 25
    Anglo-Saxon values of, 17-20
    Christian background of, 16, 50, 83, 111, 125

    allows for distance from heroic society, 61-62
    suggested by references to God/Bible, 15
    and view of pagan limitations, 84-85
    as didactic, 74
    learning of, 24-25
    talent of, 119
  as Christian apologetic, 88
  compared with Homer's works, 14, 50, 70, 87
    emphasis on hospitality, 41
    heroic ideals of, 32
    as primary epic, 35
  date of, 83
  as epic, 34
  as heroic elegy, 29
  historical background of, 16-19, 31-32, 104-105, 126-28
    and Anglo-Saxon rulers, 43-44
    and fall of Roman Empire, 16, 31
    and Germanic migrations, 38
    and Germanic traditions, 45, 46, 47, 48, 50-51
    see also Anglo-Saxon culture; *Beowulf,* author of; Old English literature
  as historical poem, 24, 46, 126, 127
    alluding to old tales, 25, 45, 125
  as key to Anglo culture, 37
  new interpretations of, 89-90

origins of, 14, 36
  and handwritten copy, 15
  respect for ancestors, 16
success of, 28
  see also characters; structure;
    themes
Beowulf, as hero, 20-21, 27, 79,
    81
  burial of, 43-44, 62, 72, 115
    as foreshadowed by Scyld
      Scefing funeral, 125
    in memorial mound by sea,
      62, 71, 80
  Christian, 19, 36, 65
    and agent of God, 85-86
    is free of pagan curse, 70
    is prepared to die, 97
  death of, 69, 72-73
    as climax of poem, 80
    speech while dying, 68, 84
  and decision to fight dragon,
    60, 63, 65, 66, 92
    as allegory of humanity's
      fall, 67, 68
    as arrogant, 21-22, 62, 71
    as courageous, 69, 73, 93, 94,
      97
    and foreboding/doubt, 51,
      70, 80, 84
    is foreshadowed by song,
      125-26
    as selfish, 64
  dignity/nobility of, 95, 97, 120
  is based on Germanic legend,
    16
  and king, 22, 44, 56
    with heroic fault, 62, 106
    of peace, 96
    as new type of, 78
  overthrown, 48
  pagan, 19, 25
    limitations of, 87-88, 119
  pride of, 59, 65-66, 78-79
  as restorer of order, 102-103
  unknown marital status of, 50
  see also characters; Geats, the
Bible, 21, 61, 117
  Cain and Abel story, 15, 116
  Genesis, 24
  Old Testament history, 119

Bloomfield, M.W., 62
Boethius, 53
Bolton, W.F., 89
Boniface, Saint, 104
Bonjour, Adrien, 108, 125
British Museum, 15

Caedmon, 36, 105
Camargo, Martin, 112
Chance, Jane, 107
characters
  cowardly retainers of Be-
    owulf, 40, 60, 70, 71, 93
    as danger to realm, 96-97
    Germanic revulsion for, 123
    as ignored by Beowulf, 122
    as not legally culpable, 106
  Hrothgar, 17, 27, 44, 103, 121
    and Beowulf's farewell, 50
    as builder of Heorot, 101,
      128
    failing strength/helplessness
      of, 76, 77, 85, 93
    as ideal king, 61, 75
    as negated by Grendel, 102
    praises Beowulf, 58, 65
    restraint of, 60
    sermon of, 74, 86, 107
      inspired by Beowulf's
        sword hilt, 78
      warning Beowulf against
        pride, 35, 59, 61
  Hygelac, 19, 50, 60, 92, 116
    court celebration of, 107
    fall of, 28, 29
    is referred to in historical
      documents, 127
    and opposition to Beowulf's
      expedition, 59
  Unferth, 50, 121, 122, 124
  Wiglaf, 40, 80, 84, 93, 95
    on Beowulf's decision to
      fight dragon, 60, 63, 69, 71
    as destiny, 92
    as doomed, 85, 87
    as heroic, 65, 127
    as mistaken, 61, 91-92
    and rebuke to retainers, 70,
      106, 122, 123
    as untried warrior, 62, 94

see also Beowulf, as hero; Grendel; women

Chaucer, Geoffrey, 61

Chickering, Howell D., Jr., 20, 38

Church of England, 15

Consolation of Philosophy (Boethius), 53

Cotton, Sir Robert, 15

Cultural World in Beowulf, The (Hill), 95

Digressions in Beowulf (Bonjour), 125

Dodds, E.R., 50

dragon, 22, 40, 48, 69-70, 107
  as agent of fate, 30, 60
  arousal of, 57
  compared to Grendel, 21, 58, 103
  as danger to kingdom, 72
  as mythical element, 127
  as symbol of challenge, 22
  and treasure, 64-65, 71, 96
  as worthy opponent for Beowulf, 29
  see also Beowulf, as hero; characters; imagery

Dream of the Rood, 36

Earl, James W., 47

Ecclesiastical History (Bede), 43, 124

Eliot, T.S., 125

Gang, T.M., 57

Garmonsway, G.N., 94

Geats, the, 29, 43-44, 47, 52, 70
  at Beowulf's funeral, 115
  destruction of, 17, 22, 62, 63
    Beowulf not responsible for, 73, 96, 128
    as historical fact, 127
    as result of Beowulf's actions, 56
    was predicted, 71, 80, 104
  and failure to live by heroic ideal, 96-97
  identification of audience with, 28, 124

as opposed to fight with dragon, 93

Goldsmith, Margaret E., 20, 22, 63, 91, 96

Greeks and the Irrational, The (Dodds), 50

Greenfield, Stanley B., 65

Grendel, 24, 29, 59, 119, 121
  defeat of, 125, 126
  as high point of poem, 113
  as descendant of Cain, 21, 48, 58, 86, 123
  and enemy of God, 56
  and envious of joy, 48, 57, 100-101, 128
  and hostility of natural world toward, 100
  and kinslayer, 76
  as evil incarnate, 57
  and fens, 52
  mother of, 35, 47, 86, 115, 122
    as avenger, 57, 58, 113
    as contrasted with feminine ideal, 108-109, 110
    and structure of poem, 107, 111
  see also dragon; imagery

Halverson, John, 99

Henry VIII, 15

Heorot hall, 17, 24, 27, 57, 71
  as center of narrative structure, 102-103
  destruction of, 121
  as major symbol of poem, 75
  as object of Grendel's spite, 21, 77-78, 102, 105
  as representative of civilization, 99-101, 105
  and center of society, 14, 99
  and hospitality, 41
  and order, 53
  and symbol of social unity, 32
  as supreme artifact, 106
  as symbol of regality/purity, 76-77

Hieatt, A. Kent, 45

Hill, John M., 95, 116

Historia Francorum (Gregory
of Tours), 127
Huppé, Bernard F., 20, 82
Hymn to the Creation (Caedmon), 35

imagery, 52, 102
  arms and armor, 78
    Beowulf's sword hilt, 59, 78,
      86
    as defense against nature, 53
    sword as motif, 60, 127
  monsters, 19, 21, 29-30
    as antitypes of Germanic
      ideal, 111
    as representation of evil, 76,
      79
  and symbolism of dragon's
    hoard, 33, 67, 85
  see also dragon; Grendel;
    Heorot hall
*Images of Community in Old
English Poetry* (Magennis),
105
Irving, Edward B., 21

Jackson, W.T.H., 66

Kittredge, George Lyman, 72
Klaeber, Frederick, 89, 92

language, 14, 30, 32, 39, 53
  alliteration, 34
  Anglo-Saxon roots of, 37
  meter, 27, 28
  patterns, 56
  see also structure
Lewis, C.S., 50
Leyerle, John, 22, 56, 90, 91, 96

Magennis, Hugh, 105, 120
Middle Ages, 31
Milton, John, 35
Mitchell, Bruce, 22

Niles, John D., 89

Ogilvy, J.D.A., 17, 69
Old English literature, 34, 38-
  39, 46, 72, 75

contrasted with Middle English, 36-37
and foundations of Anglo-
  American culture, 32
fusing of heroic/Christian values in, 39
pathos of, 104
sense of mortality in, 105
see also themes
oral tradition, 15, 24, 33, 41
  loss of, 38
  and praise, 58
  and primary epic, 34-35

Raw, Barbara, 89
Robinson, Fred C., 19, 49
Rousseau, Jean-Jacques, 52

Schücking, L.L., 63, 64
Scyldings, the, 26, 75, 77-78,
  113, 122
  are destroyed by treason, 28
  and Germanic kingship, 74
Seafarer, The, 39
Shakespeare, William, 53, 81
*Sir Gawain and the Green
Knight*, 61
structure, 25-27, 28, 59, 107,
  111
  digressions in, 125, 126
    for atmospheric effect, 127-
      28
    and Finn episode, 109, 112-13
  in second half of poem, 28, 70,
    79, 85, 118
    as inferior to first half, 72
    influence of Christianity on,
      83, 84
    questions raised by, 82
  and technique of interlace
    narrative, 61
  see also language
Swanton, Michael, 14, 16, 74

Tacitus, 39, 41, 123
Tharaud, Barry, 31
themes, 19, 104
  contradictory values, 56, 60
    heroic vs. Christian, 36, 70,
      73, 90, 115-17

and condemnation of
heroic values, 20, 83-85,
91
glory vs. salvation, 62,
87-88
in hero's dying speech, 68
revenge vs. forgiveness,
86-87
shame vs. guilt, 50-51
ideals vs. weakness, 124
contrast of sorrow/feasting,
113
contrast of youth/death, 27
courage, 34
defeat, 28
exile, 39
fate, 53, 78, 81, 87
fear of destruction, 103
hospitality, 41, 99
giving of gifts, 39, 51-52
loyalty, 45, 109, 116-17
and kinship, 40-41, 75, 106
between men, 43, 46-47,
50
failure of, 121-24
to one man, 39-40, 104-105
natural world as threat, 52,
53
paternalism, 71
pessimism, 121
pre-Christian, 24, 25
pride, 72, 81
revenge, 40, 46-47, 95
and blood feuds, 116, 126

Christian condemnation of,
86
organized/legal, 51
and tolerance of church, 42
as vicious cycle, 87, 117-18
transience of power, 79-80
see also Anglo-Saxon culture;
Beowulf, as hero; Heorot
hall
Thinking About Beowulf (Earl),
47
Tolkien, J.R.R., 24, 57, 91

Vikings, 38
Virgil, 35

Wanderer, The, 39
Whitelock, Dorothy, 42
women, 49, 126
in Anglo-Saxon society, 41-43
Hildeburh, 109, 110, 112
as focus of recent scholarship, 113
as tragic victim, 114
as peace-bringers, 42, 108-
109, 115, 118
doomed to fail, 110
Queen Wealhtheow, 52, 99,
122
as creator of harmony, 115
suffering of, 114-15
see also characters
Wright, David, 125

11/05   16   8/05
9/0 8 (20)
      5/16 (32) 2/16